I0107559

ANALYSIS

PALEY'S PRINCIPLES

OF

MORAL AND POLITICAL

PHILOSOPHY.

By C. V. LE GRICE. A. M.

THE SIXTH EDITION.

UT EA RATIONE ET DISTRIBUTIONE SUB UNO ASPECTU PONERENTUR.
CICERONIS FRAGMENTA.

SOLD BY M. JONES, NEWGATE-STREET; T. CONDER,
BUCKLERSBURY; D. EATON, HIGH HOLBORN, LONDON;
AND J. DEIGHTON, AND J. NICHOLSON,
CAMBRIDGE.

1811.

[*Price Two Shillings and Sixpence.*]

LATELY PUBLISHED,

New Editions of the following Works.

Analysis of Paley's Evidences of Christianity.   Price 2s. 6d.

A Complete Analysis or Abridgment of Paley's Evidences of Natural Theology.   Price 3s. 6d.

A Syllabus of Locke's Essay on the Human Understanding. Price 1s. 6d.

A Complete Analysis or Abridgment of Dr. Adam Smith's Wealth of Nations.   Price 6s. boards.

MORAL PHILOSOPHY,

Is the Science, which teaches men their duty, and the reasons of it. B. 1. c. 1.

The Rules of Life may be deficient, or ill-applied.

These Rules are the Law—of Honour—of the Land, —of Scripture.

The *First* being constructed by people of fashion to facilitate their intercourse with one another, favours whatever indulgencies of the passions does not interrupt that intercourse. B. 1. c. 2.

It regulates the duties only betwixt equals.

Omits those to the Supreme Being, and inferiors.

The *Second* omits duties which are not objects of compulsion. B. 1. c. 3. s. 1.

Permits to go unpunished crimes which cannot be defined. S. 2.

If otherwise, it would be inconsistent with freedom.

The *Third* contains General Rules of Piety. B. 1. c. 4.

Particular instances useless because innumerable.

It presupposes a knowledge of Natural Justice.

The object of the Scriptures is to enforce practice by new sanctions, and a greater certainty.

Hence they do not supersede the use of this Science, nor, their end being considered, are they imperfect.

Moral Sense, B. 1. c. 5.

Whether it exists cannot be found by experiment.
Arguments for its existence.

1st. We approve or disapprove certain actions without deliberation.

2d. This approbation or disapprobation is uniform and universal.

A 2

Against it, 1st. This uniformity of sentiment does not pervade all nations.

2d. Approbation of particular conduct arises from a sense of its advantages.

The idea continues when the motive no longer exists.

Receives strength from authority, imitation, &c.

The efficacy of imitation is most observable in children.

3d. There are no maxims universally true, but bend to circumstances.

4th. There can be no idea without an object, and instinct is inseparable from the idea of the object.

No dependence on the Moral Sense in reasoning, because scarcely distinguishable from prejudice and habit.

Could carry with it no authority, because every man would be his own judge.

Human Happiness.

Happy is a relative term.   B. 1. c. 6.

Happiness does not consist in

1st. Pleasures of Sense,

Because they are of short duration at the time;

Because they cloy by repetition;

Because eagerness for intense delights takes away relish for others.

These objections are valid independent of loss of health, &c.

2d. In exemption from evils which are without, as labour, &c.

Because the mind must be employed.

Hence pain is sometimes a relief to the uneasiness of vacuity.

3d. In greatness or elevated station,

Because the highest in rank are not happiest, and so in proportion.

Because superiority, where there is no competition, is seldom contemplated.

Happiness is to be judged of by the apparent happiness of mankind, which consists in

1st. The exercise of the social affections.

2d. The exercise of the faculties of body or mind for an engaging end.

Because there is no happiness without something to hope for.

Those pleasures are most valuable, which are most productive of engagement in the pursuit.

Therefore endeavours after happiness in a future state produce greatest happiness in this world.

3d. In a prudent constitution of habits.

Habits of themselves are much the same, because what is habitual becomes nearly indifferent;

Therefore those habits are best, which allow of indulgence in the deviation from them.

Hence that should not be chosen as a habit, which ought to be refreshment.

Hence by a perpetual change the stock of happiness is soon exhausted.

4th. In health.

Because necessary for the enjoyment of every pleasure.

Because itself is a pleasure, perhaps the sole happiness of some animals.

From the above account follow two conclusions.

1st. Happiness appears to be pretty equally distributed.

2d. Vice has no advantage over Virtue with respec to this world's happiness.

VIRTUE is

" The doing good to mankind, in obedience to the wil
" of God, and for the sake of everlasting happiness.
B. 1. c. 7.

It may be divided into duties towards God, towards others, and towards ourselves.

General Observations.

1st. Mankind act more from habit than reflection. B. 1. c. 7.

We know it from experience.

This mode of acting best suits the exigencies of life·

Therefore Virtue consists in forming proper habits.

Hence whatever tends to a good habit is to be done for that reason, and *vice versa*.

2d. The Christian religion has not ascertained the precise quantity of virtue necessary to salvation;

Because impossible to be expressed or limited.

Hence rewards and punishments will be in proportion to our deeds.

These General Positions may be advanced.

1st. A state of happiness cannot be expected by those who are conscious of no moral or religious rule;

Because, if so, religion, both natural and moral, would be useless.

2d. By those, who reserve to themselves the practice of any particular sin;

Because all commands stand alike on the authority of God.

Because such allowance would tolerate every vice.

Because Scripture excludes such hope.

3d. A state of unprofitableness will be punished;

Because so laid down in Scripture.

4th. Where a question of conduct is doubtful, we are bound to take the safe side;

Because—" Whatsoever is not of faith is sin."

Moral Obligation.

Moralists all coincide in prescribing the same rules of conduct, but differ in the reasons why we are obliged to pursue such conduct. B. 2. c. 1.

A man is *obliged* when he is urged by a violent motive resulting from the command of another. B. 2. c. 3.

Why am I obliged to keep my word? B. 2. c. 3.

Because urged by a violent motive (fear of punishment after death) resulting from the command of another. (God.)

N. B. Punishments after death taken for granted. B. 2. c. 3. s. 2.

To inquire what is our duty is to inquire what *is the* will of God. B. 2. c. 4.

Which may be found,

1st. By his express declaration in scripture.

2d. By the light of nature.

By which inquiring into the tendency of an action to promote or diminish the general happiness, we find the will of God, B. 2. c. 4.

N. B. Actions are to be considered here in the abstract. Note, c. 6.

The Divine Benevolence.

God wishes the happiness of man. B. 2. c. 5.

For he did not wish man's misery;

Because he might have made every object offensive, which he has not.

He was not indifferent about it;

Because, if so, all things came by chance.

The world is full of contrivances, which shew design,

These contrivances for beneficial purposes;

Liable to evil, but not constructed for that purpose.

Utility.

Whatever is expedient is right. B. 2. c. 6.

The utility of a moral rule constitutes the obligation of it.

This is to be judged of by general rules. B. 2. c. 7.

Because actions are expedient or not according to their general consequences. B. 2. c. 8.

Of Right.

Right and obligation are reciprocal, B. 2. c. 9.

Therefore right signifies " consistent with the will of God." C. 9. and 4.

Right is a quality of persons or of actions. C. 9.

Rights of persons are Natural or Adventitious, Alienable, or Unalienable, Perfect or Imperfect. C. 10.

Natural Rights would belong to a man, although no civil government subsisted, as right to life, &c.

Adventitious would not, as right of a General over his soldiers, &c.

Some Rights are alienable, as of property, &c. C. 10. s. 2.

Some unalienable, as of husband over wife, &c.

Rights are perfect, which may be asserted by force, as right to life, &c. C. 10. s. 3.

Imperfect may not, as right of a benefactor to gratitude, &c.

Because indeterminate.

Therefore to assert them by force is inconsistent with the general happiness, that is, the will of God. B. 2. c. 4.

Imperfection of a right refers only to force in assertion, not at all to the obligation of a right.

General Rights of mankind are those, which belong to the species collectively. B. 2. c. 11.

These are,

1. A right to the fruits of the earth.   S.

Because provided for us by God.

2. A right to the flesh of animals.   S. 2.

Because given by authority of God for support of life.

Therefore all waste or misapplication of them a sin.

Hence nothing should be exclusive property, which can conveniently be common, and *vice versa*.

3. The right of extreme necessity.   S. 3.

As a right to use or destroy another's property, if necessary to our preservation.

Because Division of Property was not instituted to operate to the destruction of any.

Institution of Property.   B. 3. c. 2.

Advantages of it.

Increases the produce of the earth.   S. 1.

Preserves it to maturity.   S. 2.

Prevents contests.   S. 3.

Improves convenincy of living.   S. 4.

Right of Property in Land.

Not founded on the tacit consent of mankind. B. 3. c.4.

Because silence is not consent where a person knew nothing about the matter.

Not founded on labour being mixed with it ;

Because this is just, only when the value of the labour is proportional to the value of the thing, or where the thing derives its value from the labour.

This plea will not give right in perpetuity ;

Nor will it hold in taking possession of a tract of land as a navigator.

The first right of ownership arises from the natural right of man to appropriate to his own use what he stands in need of.   B. 2. c. 10. s. 1.—B. 3. c. 4.

B

This will justify property only as far as a provision for natural exigencies.

The real foundation of our right is the " Law of the Land." B. 3. c. 4.

Property is established by the will of God. B. 3. c. 2.

Land cannot be divided into property without the regulation of the Law of the Land. B. 3. c. 4.

Therefore so to regulate it is " consistent with the will of God."

Hence right to property in land does not depend on the manner of the original acquisition, or on the expediency of the law.

Of these principles a bad use *may* be made :

But he is guilty in *foro conscientiæ,* who abides not by the spirit of the law.

N. B. Property may be regarded as the principal subject of the determinate relative duties.

Promises. B. 3. c. 5.

The obligation of them arises from the necessity of it to the well-being and existence of society. S. 1.

They are to be interpreted in the sense in which the promiser was conscious the promisee received them. S. 2.

Because in any other sense they would be equivocal.

Hence the obligation depends on the expectations excited.

Therefore tacit promises are binding.

Promises are not binding.

1st. Where the performance is impossible. S. 3.

If the promiser knows this at the time of promise, he raises an expectation which he knows he cannot gratify, that is, breaks a promise.

2d. Where the performance is unlawful ;

Because the promiser was under a prior obligation to the contrary.

This holds whether the unlawfulness was known to the parties at the time of the promise, or not.

The reward of a sin, when committed, ought to be paid;

Because performance of the promise does not increase the sin.

A promise is binding, if it be lawful, when demanded, though it was not so at the time of promising.

A promise is not unlawful, when it produces no effect beyond what would have taken place, had the promise never been made;

Because the public lose nothing by the promise, when they could have gained nothing without it.

3d. Where they contradict a former promise;

Because the performance is then unlawful.

4th. Before acceptance.

Because no expectation has been voluntarily excited.

5th. Which are released by promisee.

6th. In certain cases, where they are erroneous.

7th. Which were made in fear.

Because the general consequences would be hurtful to mankind.

Vows are under the same laws as promises.

Although the violation of them shews want of reverence to the Supreme Being; the performance of them where they become unlawful, shews greater.

A Contract is a mutual promise. B. 3. c. 6.

Therefore is to be interpreted in the same manner.

Contracts of Sale. C. 7.

The seller is bound to discover the faults of what he sells;

Because the buyer did not expect them. C. 6.

Passing bad money is an article of this kind.

The tradesman is bound to sell at market price;

Because so expected by the buyer. C 6.

Innumerable cases must be determined by *custom*;

Because the contracting parties tacitly include the rules of customs as conditions of sale.

Contracts of Hazard.

No advantage is to be taken on either side, which was not expected by the other. C. 6.

Contracts of lending of Property;

Which is divided into inconsumable (i. e. where the thing lent is itself to be returned) and consumable, (i. e. which can be returned only in kind) as corn, money &c.

If the thing lent be lost or damaged, who is to bear the loss?

Where the owner foresees the risk, he undertakes it;

Because an implied condition of the contract. B. 3. c. 6.

If an estate, during a lease, be altered in its value, the hirer takes the consequences only of those alterations, which might be expected by the parties. C. 6.

Contracts concerning the lending of Money.
B. 3. c. 10.

The prohibition in Scripture against usury was meant only for the Jews.

Usury, that is, interest according to the will of the lender, is agreeable to natural equity.

It is necessary that it should be under regulations, as by that means it will contribute to general happiness;

Because it checks the accumulation of wealth without industry.

Because it enables men to adventure in trade.

Because it enables the state to borrow.

Money borrowed in one country and paid in another, is to be paid so that the lender is not the sufferer. C. 6.

So if the value of coin be altered.

A man is bound to pay money, when any lawful method is in his power;

Because on this security credit was given. B. 3. c. 6.

Imprisonment of insolvent debtors is just, being a public punishment for a crime. B. 3. c. 10. B. 2. c. 8.

Properly put in the power of the creditor, because he
is most likely to be vigilant, and because it adds to his
security.

It is unjust in the creditor to imprison an unfortunate
debtor;

Because he punishes, where there is no crime according to the spirit of the law.

Contracts of Service. B. 3. c. 11.

The Master's authority extends no farther than the
terms of the contract will justify.

Contracts of Service are subject to the same laws as
promises are.

Rules of custom are tacit conditions of the contract.

The master is responsible for every thing done by a
servant under the general authority committed to him.

Because people act with the servant under this expectation.

To give a bad servant a good character is criminal.

The reverse of this is equally, if not more criminal.

A master is obliged to check vice in his domestics;

Because he has authority, which he is ordered by
Scripture to use for that purpose.

Contracts of Labour.

Commissions. B. 3. c. 12.

Whoever undertakes another's business, promises to
employ the same care upon it as if it were his own, and
no more.

These cases are subject to the same laws as promises
are. *Vide* b. 3. c. 5.

14

Partnership. C. 13.

Binding in the same respects as all contracts, that is, promises.

Division of stock must depend on custom or agreement.

According to natural equity the profits should be divided between the labouring partner, and him who provides money, in the proportion of interest of money to the wages of labour.

Offices. C. 14.

In offices, as fellowships of colleges, &c. a man performs his duty who performs what his electors expected of him.

Because this was the expectation on both sides at the time of contract.

An Office may *not* be discharged by deputy,

1st. Where confidence is reposed in the particular abilities of the person elected.

2d. Where the custom hinders.

3d. Where the duty from its nature cannot be so well performed by a deputy.

4th. Where to employ deputies from general consequences would be bad, as in the army.

Non-residence of parochial clergy does not fall under these heads.

Revenues of the church are a common fund for the support of the national religion.

So to be judged of in its distribution.

Lies. C. 15.

A Lie is a breach of promise; because in discourse there is a tacit promise to speak the truth.

The general consequences of lying are bad:

Because confidence is necessary to the intercourse of society..

Hence " white lies" are not entirely innocent.

(They habitually lead to others of a darker complexion.)

Hence too, *pious* frauds, though meant to do good, are highly injurious to the cause of religion.

There are falsehoods which are not lies, and therefore not criminal.

1st. Where no one is deceived, as in novels, &c.

2d. Where no inconvenience results from the want of confidence in such cases; as where you tell a falsehood to a madman, a robber, &c.

Upon this principle we may deceive an enemy by feints, spies, &c. in war.

But by no means in treaties, truces, &c.

Any wilful deceit is a lie.

A man may *act* a lie.

There are lies of omission, as where you conceal part of the truth.

Oaths. C. 16.

Forms of Oaths vary in different countries. S. 1.

The signification is the same, viz. the calling of God to witness. S. 2.

Our Saviour's words concerning oaths relate not to judicial, but wanton oaths. S. 3.

Oaths receive their obligations from a belief that God will punish perjury, which we have reason to think he will. S. 4.

1. Because the perjurer implies a disbelief of God's power or contempt of it.

2. Because perjury violates a superior confidence, and therefore it is hurtful in its general consequences.

Hence a Quaker's word, if broken, incurs the guilt of perjury.

Promissory oaths are not binding where the promise would not be. *Vide.* B. 3. c. 5.

An oath is designed for the security of the imposer, therefore it is just "*jurare in animum imponentis.*"

Oaths in Evidence. C. 17.

The witness swears to speak the whole truth:
Therefore to conceal part is perjury.

This oath is not binding in some cases according to the law of the land, that is, *animus imponentis.*

Oath of Allegiance. C. 18.

Ascertains not the extent of the subject's obedience, but the person to whom it is due.

The oath excludes,

1. All intention to support the claim of another.

2. All design, at the time, of deposing the reigning prince.

3. All opposition from private views.

It permits

1. Resistance to the king, if beneficial to the community.

2. Disobedience to unlawful commands.

3. Does not require allegiance after he is deposed.

Oath against Simony. C. 20.

Was meant to restrain the patron of a piece of preferment from being influenced in his choice of a presentee by a bribe, or any benefit to himself.

The law determines what is a simoniacal contract.

1st. Purchasing a benefice already vacant.

2d. A clergyman purchasing the next turn of a benefice for himself, directly or indirectly.

3d. The procuring of any preferment by ceding to the patron any right or portion of profit.

4th. A bond to resign upon demand.

Oath to observe local Statutes. C. 21.

The *animus imponentis*, that is, the measure of the juror's duty, seems to be satisfied, when nothing is omitted, but what from change of circumstances the founder, it may be presumed, would have dispensed with.

To come within this rule, the inconveniency must be manifest by being unlawful, impracticable or prejudicial to the end of the institution.

Subscription to Articles of Religion. C. 22.

The subscribers assent is governed by the same rule of interpretation as oaths are, that is, the *animus imponentis.*

The imposer, whose intention is to be satisfied, is the legislature of the 13th. Eliz.

It is impossible that the legislature could expect the assent of ten thousand men, and that in perpetual succession, to many hundreds of controverted propositions.

The intention was to exclude from offices in the church,

1. All abettors of popery.

2. Anabaptists, at that time a powerful party on the continent.

3. The puritans, who were hostile to an episcopal constitution.

4. In general the members of such leading sects, or foreign establishments as threatened to overthrow our own.

Some limitations of the patron's choice may be necessary to prevent unedifying contentions between neighbouring teachers, or between the teachers and their congregations.

This danger, if it exist, might be obviated by converting the articles of faith into articles of peace.

c

Wills. C. 23.

The disposal by will of the produce of personal labour is a natural right;

Because there is no limit to the continuance of the right.

With respect to other property, as of land, the right is adventititous;

1. Because at the death of the possessor his want of it ceaseth. *Vide* B. 3. c. 4.

2. Because if a man possesses any right of disposal, he possesses a right of disposal for ever, which is absurd.

Therefore this right is received from, and is to be regulated by, the law of the land.

Hence, if informal, the will is not binding;

Because the conditions, upon which the right was obtained, were not complied with.

Succession to intestates must be regulated by the law of the land.

There are many *imperfect duties* in respect to the making and observing of Wills. *Vide,* B. 1. c. 3. s. 1.

Such as respect to the intention of the deceased,

Impartial love of children, &c.

Provision for poor relatives.

Charity. C. 3. c. 1. p. 2.

Is the promoting of the happiness of our inferiors, of doing which there are three principal methods:

First method. By tender treatment of our domestics and dependants. C. 2.

It is our interest; for they will shew their gratitude by being serviceable, and our obligation to them is much greater than theirs to us.

It is our duty; because we are forbid to diminish the sum of human happiness.

All uneasiness therefore, which we occasion without a just cause is wrong.

The same is applicable to Slaves;

Because founded on a principle independent of the contract of service.

Slavery. C. 3.

Is an obligation to labour for another without consent of the servant.

This may arise from crimes, captivity, or debt.

The continuance ought to be in proportion to the crime.

The Slave Trade can be excused by none of these principles.

The necessity pleaded for it is ridiculous.

The christian scriptures interfere with no civil institution, and therefore not with slavery.

If they had a *bellum servile* might have ensued.

This does not argue against a gradual emancipation.

2d. Method. By professional assistance. B. 2. c. 4.

This kind of beneficence is chiefly to be expected from members of the legislature, magistrates, legal, and sacerdotal professions.

Because the law cannot provide for the poor in these cases, and the rich can take care of themselves.

Every professional man has it in his power to do the greatest good at the least expence.

3d. Method. By pecuniary bounty, C. 5.

We are obliged to bestow relief on the poor. S. 1.

(The impulse we feel indicates the divine intention.)

1. Because property was divided that all might have a sufficiency. *Vide*, B. 2. c. 4.

2. Because that scripture enjoins to bestow relief.

The manner of bestowing it. S. 2.

c 2

It is better to give a considerable sum among few than the same sum among many.

To give to public charities is eminently useful, because in them money goes farther.

Indiscriminate relief to beggars is not to be encouraged.

That charity is most useful, which promotes industry.

Charity is not to be kept secret, if by being published it may be useful in influencing others.

Few excuses for not giving relief are just. S. 3.

Resentment.

May be distinguished into anger and revenge, B. 3. c. 6.

Anger is involuntary in some degree. C. 7.

Therefore, if checked, is no crime.

Is sinful, if it is suffered to continue long.

This is the doctrine of scripture.

Reflections, which may appease it, are numerous.

Revenge. C. 8.

Is the infliction of pain on another in consequence of an injury received from him, farther than the just ends of reparation or punishment require.

Is forbidden by scripture, which forbids the neglect even of imperfect duties towards an enemy.

At the same time the punishment of public offenders is permitted;

Because necessary to public happiness.

So, if it be from a good motive, correction of vice is proper in individuals.

It is productive of good.

Witness the seclusion of bad women from the company of women of character.

Duelling. C. 9.

As a punishment absurd;

Because the person offended may be the sufferer.

So also as a reparation;

Because it does not undo the injury.

It is complied with for the sake of fashion.

Regard for reputation will not justify murder.

In expostulating with the duellist, we have a right to suppose his adversary to fall;

Because if he has no right to kill, he has no right to attempt it.

Where the injury is forgiven, and both parties fight for reputation's sake, there is no distinction between the guilt of him who accepts, and him who gives the challenge.

The law on this head is insufficient;

But opinion cannot be controlled by civil institutions; therefore a Court of Honour, or something similar, seems the only remedy.

Litigation. C. 10. p. 2.

Is not inconsistent with any rule of the gospel, when it is instituted with a view to the public good, or with a view to the end of justice and safety.

It becomes unjust when instituted from any other motive, and when it is carried on in any manner that does not most readily promote these ends.

It is our duty to bring an offender to punishment, when it is conducive to the public good.

Gratitude. C. 11.

Is a duty, because the violation of it would be pernicious in its general consequences;

Because the love of God cannot exist without it,

It does not supersede other duties.

Slander. C. 12.

Slander is the producing of gratuitous mischief.

Speaking is acting, if the mischief and motive are the same.

Truth may be instrumental to the success of malice.

If the end is bad so are the means.

The guilt must be measured by the misery produced.

The guilt of inconsiderate slander consists in want of regard to general consequences;

Therefore shews want of just affection for human happiness.

Of Relative Duties, which result from the Constitution of the Sexes. B. 3. p. 3.

The constitution of the sexes is the foundation of marriage.

Collateral to the subject are fornication, seduction, adultery, incest, polygamy, divorce.

Consequential to it are the reciprocal duties of parent and child.

Use of Marriage Institutions. C. 1.

They promote

1st. The private comfort of individuals; especially of females.

Whatever promotes the happiness of the majority, is binding upon the whole.

2. The better production of children, and provision for them.

3d. The peace of society.

4th. The better government of society. S. 4. and 5.

5th. The encouragement of industry.

Fornication. C. 2.

The guilt of it consists in,

1st. Its tendency to diminish the number of marriages.

2d. Encouragement of prostitution and its miseries.

3d. Encouragement of habits of lewdness.

Consequently it incurs the guilt of the general consequences of lewdness.

4th. The perpetuation of a loathsome disease.

It is expressly forbid by Scripture.

Licensed brothels vitiate the public opinion.

The keeping of a mistress is not the same as marriage, because not so beneficial to the woman and her children.

Is a crime;

1st. Because it is fornication.

2d. Because it is pernicious in its general consequences. B. 2. c. 8.

Seduction. C. 3.

Is a fraud of which the injury is threefold.

1st. To the woman, who suffers the pain of shame, and sustains the loss of her reputation, and generally of her moral principle.

The evils arising to the woman in consequence are great, and the seducer incurs the guilt of them.

2d. To the family.

3d. To the public, who lose a valuable member of society.

Adultery. C. 4.

Where the man solicits the chastity of the woman, he incurs the guilt of seduction in every respect.

The crime of both parties is aggravated by the extreme misery brought upon the husband, and children.

The guilt is independent of discovery, because such conduct is pernicious in its general consequences.

And is a breach of the marriage vow before God.

Prior transgression of either party is no justification;

Because the marriage vow does not depend on reciprocal fidelity.

The Scripture makes a difference between fornication and adultery.

Christ's opinion of the magnitude of the sin cannot be inferred from his words to the adulterous woman.

He told her, she had " sinned."

Incest. C. 5.

Should be kept in utter abhorrence to preserve chastity in families.

Restrictions extending to remove degrees of kindred are founded on positive laws,

Which are justifiable because beneficial in their general consequences in diffusing wealth, &c.

Polygamy. C. 6.

May be judged to be against the will of God.

Because he has created very nearly equal numbers of each sex.

And because it is hurtful in its general consequences.

For 1st. It distracts the affections.

2d. It dissolves the vigour of the faculties.

3d. It debases half the creation.

4th. It provides less for the children.

It produces no benefit in population.

The words of Christ, whosoever putteth away his " wife, and marrieth another, committeth adultery," imply a prohibition of it.

It is retained only where christianity is not professed.

Divorce. C. 7.

By Divorce is meant the dissolution of the Marriage contract at the will of the husband.

If it be by mutual consent, it is equally liable to objection.

Except on account of the duties, which parents owe to their children, there is no reason *in nature* why marriage should not be dissoluble like other contracts.

General consequences require that it should be indissoluble;

1. Because it tends to preserve concord between the parties.

2. Because new objects of desire would continually be sought after, if men could at will be released from the matrimonial tie.

The Law of Nature admits of an exception in favour of the injured party in cases of adultery, desertion, &c.

By no means in case of peevishness, &c. though not trivial reasons; because the unhappiness of one pair must be sacrificed to general consequences.

The Scripture allows divorce only in case of adultery. So does the Law of the Land.

Inferior causes may justify the separation of the parties, if the care of the children does not require that they should live together.

In cases of tyranny in the husband, the law provides a divorce *a mensa et thoro.*

In these cases the marriage is not dissolved, because the general consequences would be hurtful.

Sentences, which release the parties *a vinculo matrimonii,* do not dissolve a marriage; but declare that it never existed.

Marriage. C. 8.

Is a religious ceremony from custom only.

Which part should give the dowry has been settled by fashion.

As it is at present, it secures to them that assiduity and respect, which are wanted to compensate for the inferiority of their strength.

What duties the vow creates are expressed in the ceremony.

It is witnessed before God; therefore, if broken, incurs the greatest guilt of a violated oath.

Obedience on the part of the wife is ordered, because it is necessary that one party should submit.

He may conscientiously marry, who wishes and expects to entertain an affection for his wife.

The marriage vow is violated.

1st. By adultery.

2d. By behaviour, which knowingly renders the life of the other miserable.

The Law of the Land makes the consent of the parents necessary, under certain restrictions.

Duty of Parents. C. 9.

Is of great importance in the class of duties from its general consequences.

Admits of definite rules, which may be explained under the heads of

1st. Maintenance;

Because somebody must maintain the children, and parents have no right to burthen others.

Nature indicates it in the person of the mother.

The Scriptures order it.

2d. Education;

Because necessary for the child's well-being in society.

A reasonable provision for the child's happiness in respect to outward condition, which requires three things.

1st. A situation suited to his reasonable expectations and habits.

2d. A provision for that situation.

(These articles must vary with the condition of the parent.)

Hence children should be preserved in that class in which they were born, or in which others of similar expectations are accustomed to be placed.

Hence a parent is justified in making a difference in his children, according as they stand in greater or less need of his fortune from circumstances.

After their exigencies, the expectations of children may be satisfied according to primogeniture.

This point, together with general expediency, makes the difference of claim between legitimate children and bastards.

Still a parent is bound to provide for a bastard.

After a provision for exigencies, a parent may proportion his children's shares according to their behaviour.

Disinherison, nearly absolute, is justifiable only in case of utter incapability of managing an inheritance.

The third thing required in a provision for the child's happiness, is a probable security for his virtue.

This may be attained,

1st. By impressing on his mind the idea of *accountableness*.

2d. By shewing a good example,

3d. By correcting his early inclinations, and disposing of him in a situation least dangerous to his particular character.

The Rights of Parents   C. 10. b. 3. p. 3.

(That is, such as may be enforced by coercion) result from their duties.

A parent has a right to that authority, which is necessary in the exercise of his duties,

Hence a guardian has the same.

Parents have a right to choose professions for their children ;

Because it is necessary to determine before they can judge for themselves.

In competition of commands the wife here also owes obedience to her husband.

Parents have no right over the lives of their children, or to sell them into slavery.

They exceed their authority when they consult their own interest at the expence of their children's happiness.

Duty of Children. C. 11.

May be considered,

1st. During childhood.

Here the children's obedience must be implicit.

2d. After they have attained to manhood and continue in their parents' family.

Beside the general duty of gratitude to parents, they are bound to observe the regulations of the family.

3d. After they have attained to manhood and have left their father's family.

In this state the duty to parents is simply the duty of filial gratitude, which just so much exceeds other obligations, by how much a parent has been a greater benefactor than any other friend.

It requires of children to endeavour by every means to promote their parent's comfort, and to contribute to their support if they stand in need of it.

A parent has no right to destroy his children's happiness.

He has therefore no right to oppose his childrens' marriage where they have a real inclination; or to force them upon one which they dislike.

In this latter case the child must become guilty of prevarication; and parental, like all human authority, must cease, where obedience is criminal.

Nor has the parent a right to compel a child to choose a profession, to which he may be averse.

In every case the child is bound by gratitude to try earnestly, and with *sincerity*, to conquer his own inclinations, before he may act for himself.

A parent has no right to interfere, where a trust is reposed personally in the son. *Vide* B. 3. p. 2. c. 11.

The duty of children is commanded by God.

Duties to Ourselves. B. 4.

This division is retained for the sake of method.

Whether in a state of nature we may defend the most insignificant perfect right by any extremity, is very doubtful. B. 4. c. 1.

Because we cannot so easily balance between the general consequences of yielding, and the particular effect of resistance, which the person attacked is bound to do.

This right is suspended by the establishment of civil society.

Hence the individual injured is bound to submit to public arbitration.

Where it may be necessary for our preservation, all extremities are justifiable.

This is evident in a state of nature, nor is the case altered in civil society.

Because, by supposition, the laws cannot interpose to protect, nor can they compel restitution.

The defence of chastity seems to justify the same extremities.

In other cases the law of the land is our best guide.

Hence homicide in England, is justifiable;

1st. In preventing the commission of a crime, which when committed would be punishable with death.

2d. In necessary endeavours to carry the law into execution.

N. B. The rights of war are not here taken into the account.

Drunkenness. C. 2.

Casual excesses incur all, in some degree, of the guilt and danger, which attend habitual drunkenness.

We compute the guilt of it from its bad effects, which consist,

1st. In its betraying most constitutions into extravagances of anger, or sins of lewdness.

2d. It disqualifies men from the duties of their station.

3d. It is attended with expences, which can seldom be spared.

4th. It creates uneasiness to the family of the drunkard.

5th. It shortens life.

These consequences may not all meet in the same subject; but the great mischief of *example* is sure always to ensue.

It is forbidden in the Scriptures.

The guilt of any action of a drunken man bears the same proportion to the guilt of the like in a sober man, that the probability of its being the consequence of drunkenness bears to certainty.

Suicide. *B. 4. c. 3.*

Rests on this question :—" May every man who pleases " to destroy his life, innocently do so ?"

Whatever rule or limit for suicide, is assigned, must lead to a toleration of it in all cases, in which there is danger of its being committed.

The general consequences of such toleration would be

1st. The loss to the community of many valuable lives.

2d. The affliction of many families, and consternation of all.

3d. The throwing off an opportunity of meliorating our condition in a future state.

Every case must also be aggravated by particular consequences.

Scripture *implies* the sin of suicide.

1st. By speaking of human life as a *term* prescribed to us.

2d. By inculcating patience as a great virtue.

3d. By the conduct of the apostles.

The above does not argue against the right of a state over the lives of its subjects;

Because the state receives this power not from the consent of collected individuals, but from the will of God. B. 3. c. 4.

Duties towards God. B. 5.

Signify duties, of which God is the object.

Silent piety, acceptable as it is to God, does not supersede the external duties; which may be divided into worship and reverence.

Worship is made up of adoration, thanksgiving, and prayer.

Prayer comprises them all.

Of the Duty and Efficacy of Prayer, as it appears from the light of Nature. C. 2.

It is probable God expects those intreaties from us, which we naturally use to every being on whom we depend.

The same may be said of Thanksgiving.

Prayer is necessary to keep up a sense of God's agency.

The duty of prayer depends on its efficacy;

Which the perfect wisdom of the Deity does not argue against:

For he may withhold a favour unless requested by prayer:

1st. Because, on that very account, it may produce good effects on the person.

2d. Because it may encourage devotion.

3d. Because prayer has a tendency to amend the petitioner himself.

It is not necessary to devotion that the petitioner should know the circuit of causes by which his prayers may prevail.

We have no proof that inexorability is a part of that perfect wisdom, which is explained to consist in bringing about the most beneficial ends by the most beneficial means.

To say God *must* act by one, or any rule, is to assert what is beyond our comprehension.

It is no objection to the efficacy of prayer that the effects of it are not always obvious;

Because it is beneficial that they should not be.

The custom of employing one person to intercede for many is justifiable:

For the happiness of many often depends on the good offices, and why may it not on the intercessions of one individual?

Of the duty of Prayer as represented in Scripture. C. 3.

The Scriptures not only affirm the propriety of prayer in general, but furnish precepts which justify particular topics and modes of prayer.

They teach the duty and efficacy of prayer in general:

Also of prayer for particular favours by name;

Of prayer for public national blessings;

Of intercession for others;

Of the repetition of unsuccessful intreaties.

Private Prayer, Family Prayer, Public Worship. C. 4.

Each has its use, and therefore does not supersede the others.

Private prayer enables men to state wants, which cannot be the subject of public prayer. S. 1.

It is generally accompanied with more actual and solemn thoughts, which make a lasting impression.

It is particularly sanctioned by our Saviour.

Family Prayer. S. 2.

Is particularly useful from its influence upon the members of a family.

Public Worship. S. 3.

By this means a great part of mankind are instructed in religious knowledge, who would otherwise not be.

As the general consequences of the example are good, every individual is bound by the general rule to attend.

Public worship has also these advantages :

1st. It has a tendency to unite mankind together, and to enlarge the generous affections.

2d. It promotes humility in the higher, and proper dignity in the lower class of mankind, by placing them under the impression of considering their equal relation to the Deity.

Of Forms of Prayer in Public Worship. C. 5.

Liturgies not being enjoined or forbidden in scripture must be judged of by their expediency.

A Liturgy,

1st. Prevents absurd or extravagant addresses to God.

2d. It prevents the confusion of extempore prayer.

3d. It supplies in some measure the imperfections of the deliverer.

Joint prayer, which is the end of a congregation, without a Liturgy, is impossible.

Our Saviour authorises a fixed form of prayer by appointing the Lord's prayer.

The properties required in a liturgy are,

1st. That it be compendious.

Brevity may be studied too much, for it is necessary that the attention which slumbered in one part, may be recalled in another.

2d. That it express just conceptions of the divine attributes ;

Because by it the popular notions of God are formed,

3d. That it recites such wants as the congregation are likely to feel, and no other.

Upon this principle our *state* prayers are too long.

4th. That it contain as few controverted propositions as possible.

The Use of Sabbatical Institutions.   C. 6.

That seasons should be set apart for religious worship is founded on the reasons that make worship a duty.

That they be at stated intervals, and be observed by all at the same time, is easiest and best for the community.

The day appointed may be Sunday, as well as any other day.

This reasoning refers only to the time occupied in divine service.

The *manner* of the Christian Sabbath is to be defended upon its general expediency.

1st. It contributes better to the happiness of the laborious part of mankind, than any *casual* indulgencies of leisure.

(Nothing is lost by this interruption of public industry.)

2d. It leaves an opportunity for religious meditation.

3d. It gives happiness to the brute creation.

Of the Scripture Account of Sabbatical Institutions. C.7.

The Jewish Sabbath was first instituted in the wilderness.

For it is never mentioned till then, and Ezekiel and Nehemiah speak of it as being so.

The Historian in *Gen. c.* 2. writing after it was instituted, there gives the *reason* of its institution.

The Jews abstained from every kind of work, and permitted their slaves and cattle to rest; they sacrificed double sacrifice, and held holy convocations on this day.

Two questions concern the Christian Moralist:

1st. " Whether the command by which the Jewish Sabbath was instituted extends to christians ?"

It appears not;

For it seems to have been part of the peculiar law of the Jewish policy;

Because it was first immediately directed to the Jewish people alone.

The Sabbath is described as a *sign* between God and the people of Israel.

It is in its nature a ceremonial institution, like other seasons appointed by the Levitical law.

If it be binding on christians, it must bind as to the day, &c. which are not regarded.

The observance of the Sabbath is not one of the articles enjoined by the apostles in *Acts. 15th. chap.* St. Paul mentions it as a Jewish ritual.

The two objections to the command's not being of universal obligation are;

1st. The reasons given for it in the fourth commandment.

2d. Its being one of the decalogue.

These are of no weight:

The first; because different reasons were given to account for different *circumstances* in the command;

The second; because in the Scriptures, positive duties, which are of partial; and natural which are of universal obligation, are indiscriminately enumerated.

The second question is, "Whether Christ delivered " any new command upon the subject, or whether any " day was appropriated to the service of religion by the " authority or example of the apostles ?"

It appears that there was,

Because the holding of religious assemblies on the

first day of the week was so early and universal a custom in the christian church.

The Apostles seem to have practised it.

A cessation upon that day from labour was not ordered;

Because the Jews, to whom the gospel was first preached, had already a Sabbath of rest.

It does not appear that Christ or his Apostles meant the Jewish custom to be retained, the day only being changed.

From all above it appears,

That assembling upon the first day of the week for divine worship is a law of christianity;

That the resting on that day is a human institution;

Which is binding on individuals because of its beneficial general consequences;

And is recommended by its subserviency to many of the uses for which God appointed it to the Jews.

By what Acts and Omissions the Duty of the Christian Sabbath is violated. C. 8.

The duty of the day is violated by whatever opposes the uses of its institution. *Vide,* C. 6.

Wherefore it is violated,

1st. By any engagement, which hinders our attention on divine worship, or giving some time to religious meditations.

2d. By unnecessary encroachments on the rest and liberty of those, who may be under our authority.

3d. By such recreations as are usually forborne from respect to the day.

Any encroachment upon the line of distinctions in this latter instance is wrong, because pernicious in its general consequences.

Gaming, or common amusements upon this day cannot be harmless, on account of their effect upon the temper of the mind.

A sense of awe whenever the idea of the Supreme Being is presented to the thoughts, is a considerable security against vice.

It is the effect of habit.

Levity in speaking of the Deity destroys this habit.

God, perhaps for this reason, forbade the vain mention of his name.

Our Saviour extends the prohibition to every thing associated with the idea of God.

The offence of profane swearing is aggravated by the slenderness of the temptation to it.

Ridicule upon the Scriptures falls within the mischief of the law, which forbids the profanation of God's name; especially as it is extended by Christ.

That man can have little regard for his own welfare in a future state, who respects not every, the most trivial attention to it in another person.

Such is the infidel, who mocks at the superstition of the vulgar.

One unbeliever assumes the follies, which have adhered to the creed, as the doctrines of Christians, endeavouring thereby to subvert the whole system.

Another relates the vices of the sacerdotal order, endeavouring thereby to connect the character of the clergy, with the truth of christianity.

A *Third* triumphs in collecting accounts of the wars and massacres occasioned by religious zeal, as if the vices of christians were parts of christianity.

A *Fourth* displays the succession and variety of popular religions, representing christianity as the *superstition of the day.*

These men aim at victory not at truth.

Therefore can have no religious frame of mind.

They transgress the laws of reasoning and decency, and do not act honestly with mankind;

Because by matter calculated to produce effects beyond its real weight, they try to cheat men of a belief in a religion, which holds forth assurances of immortality.

The dishonesty is greater where the matter comes in the dress of insinuation, a sneer, or, as has been the case, of obscenity.

The latter works its effect independent of reason.

A sneer, who can refute?

They are both as formidable to a true religion, as a false one.

This licentiousness can scarcely be tolerable even to those men, who see *little* in christianity, supposing it to be true.

Let this class of reasoners reflect,

That if Christ had delivered no other declaration than —" The hour is coming, in the which all that are in " the graves shall hear his voice, and shall come forth ; " they that have done good, unto the resurrection of " life, and they that have done evil, unto the resurrec- " tion of damnation ;" he had pronounced a message of inestimable importance.

A future state had never before been discovered, because it never had been *proved*; and no man can prove this point, but the teacher who testifies by miracles, that his doctrine comes from God,

ELEMENTS

OF

POLITICAL KNOWLEDGE. B.

Of the Origin of Civil Government. C. 1.

GOVERNMENT at first was either Patriarchal or Military.

The order of domestic life by its manner supplied the foundation, and by the dispositions, which it generates, assisted the formation of *civil* government. § 1.

It also furnishes the first steps of the process, by which empires have been reared.

A parent would naturally retain great part of his authority, after his children were grown up, and had formed families of their own.

It is not likely, that this association, of which he was the centre of union, should altogether be dissolved upon his death.

They would still feel connected by the same habits of intercourse and affection, and by their common interests.

Experiencing inconveniences from the absence of that authority of their ancestor, they might be induced to supply his place by a choice of a formal succession;

Or might imperceptibly transfer their obedience to one of the same family, whom the parent in his life time had in some degree made partaker of his authority.

Or lastly, the prospect of those inconveniences might prompt the first ancestor to appoint a succession, which they would receive with submission.

Thus a tribe or clan became incorporated.

A second source of personal authority results from the military arrangements. § 2.

In wars men from necessity arrayed themselves under one leader, whose superiority, if he had led them with success, would not terminate with the reasons for which it was conferred.

This advantage, if it were added to the authority of a partriarchal chief, might extend, or if in the power of an ambitious and able individual, might supersede the patriarchal authority.

The causes, which have introduced hereditary dominion into reception, are chiefly the following:

The influence of association, which communicates to the son a portion of the respect, which was wont to be paid to his father.

The mutual jealousy of other competitors;

The greater envy with which all behold the exaltation of an equal, than the continuance of acknowledged authority;

The adherence of those who can preserve their own importance only by supporting the succession of the reigning prince's children;

The experienced inconveniences of election to supreme power.

Thus far the incorporation and power of clans or tribes.

Two or three of those clans were frequently, we may suppose, united by marriage, conquest, mutual defence, common distress, &c. and hence empires.

The early histories of all nations confirm the account of the origin of *civil* government.

This history affords a presumption, that the earliest governments were monarchies.

How subjection to Civil Government is maintained. C 2.

Since in all cases *the physical strength resides in the governed*, the question is, by what motives the many are induced to submit to the few.

No *single* reason will account for this general submission of men to civil government: every man has his motive, though not the same.

The subjects of a state may be divided into three distinctions of characters.

1st. They who obey from prejudice, i. e. from opinion, which is not founded upon argument.

These men are determined by an opinion of right in their governors (whatever it may be) which opinion is founded upon prescription.

The whole course of civil life favours this prejudice, for all civil rights are founded on prescription.

In all hereditary monarchies the *prescriptive title* has been more or less corroborated and augmented by an application to the religious principles of men. Hence the title of Sacred Majesty, &c. &c.

2d. They who obey from *reason*.

3d. They who obey from *self-interest.*

These men are kept in order by a satisfaction in their own enjoyments; or principally by fear of the bad consequences to themselves by resistance, which has been called *opinion of power.*

From the above principles the following cautions may be suggested to governors.

1st. To treat the general opinion with deference, because the very existence of civil authority depends on opinion.

2d. That as opinion of right is for the most part founded on *custom*, the slightest innovation in the custom of government diminishes the stability of government.

3d. Government may be too secure. Wherever this security arises from the opinion of right being predominant, it is abated merely by breaking the custom.

4th. That the physical strength does reside in the governed; and since ignorance of union and want of communication is the chief preservative to civil government, it is necessary to prevent combinations of men who are allied by the same motives and interests.

The Duty of Submission to Civil Government explained.
C. 3.

Political writers usually resolve the duty of submission to civil government into the obligation as fidelity in the performance of promises, by making a compact between the citizen and state the ground of the relation between them.

This compact is twofold.

1st. An express compact by the primitive founders of the state, who are supposed to have consented to be bound by the resolutions of the majority convened for the purpose of settling a future form of government.

This transaction has been called the Social Compact.

2d. A tacit or implied compact by all succeeding members of the state, who by accepting its protection, consent to be bound by its laws.

This account has been founded on a false supposition.

No such original convention of the people ever was held, or could be held in any country, anterior to the existence of government in that country.

Savages could not deliberate on topics, which the refinements of civil life alone could suggest.

The establishment of the United States of America was only an imitation of the social compact.

The settling the constitution, the qualifications of the constituents, the mode of electing representatives, and many important parts, were taken from old forms of government, and supposed to be already settled.

The unconstrained consent of *all* to be bound by the decision of a majority was wanting.

With regard to the implied compact, all the parties stipulating must possess the liberty of assent, or refusal, which cannot be affirmed of the subject of civil government.

Allegiance founded on the circumstance of nativity, as also the right of prohibiting subjects to depart out of the realm, are irreconcileable with this idea.

To prove the possession or acceptance of land to be a promise of allegiance, we must prove the right of the primitive inhabitants to the soil.

If this compact be a mere fiction, it is useless to argue from it; but it has been regarded as a reality, and only deserves an answer, because—

The theory leads to conclusions unfavourable to the improvement and peace of society.

1st. There must have been many points settled at the general convention called the " fundamentals of " the constitution," with which the legislature has no right to interfere, and which from their number and kind must embarrass the legislature.

2d. The subject being bound by the compact must abide by the form of government, which he finds established, be it ever so absurd, inconvenient, or unjust.

3d. Every violation of the compact on any part must absolve the obligation of the others.

From the indefinite nature of many of the obligations, this must render every form of government liable to perpetual change.

The only real ground to be assigned for the subject's obligation is—" the will of God as collected from ex-
" pediency."

" It is the will of God that the happiness of human
" life be promoted."

" Civil society conduces to that end."

" Civil societies cannot be upheld, unless, in each
" the interest of the whole society be binding on every
" part and member of it."

This conducts us to the conclusion, that—" So long
" as the interest of the whole society require it, it is the
" *will of God*, (which *will* determines our duty) that
" the established government be obeyed," and no longer.

On this principle the justice of every particular case
of resistance is reduced to a computation of the quantity of danger and grievance on one side, and of the
probability and expence of redressing it on the other.

On this point every man is a judge for himself.

For the decision cannot be referred to those whose
conduct has provoked the question.

The danger of error and abuse is no objection to the
rule of expediency, because every rule is liable to the
same or greater; and all rules which bind the conscience, must depend on private judgment.

Some important inferences result from substituting
public Expediency, in place of implied compacts, &c.

1. It may be a duty at one time to resist government
as it is at another to obey it ; viz. to resist, whenever, in
our opinion, more advantage than mischief will accrue
to the community from resistance.

2. The lawfulness of resistance does not depend alone
on the grievance sustained, but on the probable expence
and event of the contest.

3. Irregularity in the first foundation, or subsequent
injustice in getting possession of the supreme power,
are not sufficient reasons for resistance after the government is once settled.

4. Not every invasion of the constitution, or neglect

of duty in the supreme magistrate, justifies resistance, unless the consequences resulting from them are such as to outweigh the evils of civil disturbance.

Nevertheless every violation should be watched with jealousy, and resented as such, because security is weakened by every encroachment.

5. No usage or authority whatsoever is so binding, that it ought to be continued, when it may be changed with advantage to the community.

The order of succession, and some other points which are represented as the principles of the constitution, are to be approached with awe, as it is of importance that the form and usage of governing shall be acknowledged and understood, as well by governors as the governed.

6. Though the rights of all men are equal, expediency renders the civil obligations of a free people, and the subjects of absolute monarchies different.

Because, 1st. The same act of the prince is not the same grievance, where it is agreeable to the constitution and where it is not.

2d. Because redress is not equally attainable.

7. The interest of the whole is binding on every part:

As an individual cannot, neither can a province or colony justly pursue their private interest by a measure which shall appear to diminish the sum of public prosperity.

This rule must decide the question of right between Great Britain and her revolted colonies.

Of the duty of civil obedience, as stated in the Holy Scriptures. C. 4.

As to the *extent* of our civil rights and obligations Christianity has left us where she found us.

Only two passages have been alleged in the controversy, viz. *Rom.* xiii. v. 1—7. and 1. *Peter* ii. v. 13—18.

To comprehend the proper import of them, we must reflect that civil obedience involves two questions:

1st. Whether to obey government be a moral duty and obligation upon the conscience at all.

2d. How far and to what cases that obedience ought to extend.

From shewing the end, and the necessity of civil subjection, or explaining the social compact, or alleging the dictates of nature herself, we may infer, that—

"Obedience to the state is a relative duty, for the transgression of which we shall be accountable at the tribunal of divine justice, whether the magistrate be able to punish or not;" but—

The extent of this obedience requires definition and discrimination; for if public expedience be the foundation, it is also the measure, of civil obedience.

The person who revolts must compare the peril and expence of his enterprize with the effects it was intended to produce, and must make choice of the alternative by which not his own present relief or profit, but the whole and permanent interest of the state is likely to be best promoted.

This distinction is to be made with regard to the two passages above quoted from Scripture: they inculcate the duty; they do not describe the extent.

With the same absolute form of expression, the same Apostles inculcate the observance of domestic duties of servants, children, &c.

Yet no one can doubt, that the obedience of the above characters ought sometimes to be limited.

This distinction vindicates these passages of Scripture from any explanation in favour of unlimited passive obedience.

But if we consider that the first christians privately cherished an opinion, that their conversion to christianity exempted them *as of right* from the authority of the Roman Sovereign, we have more satisfactory proof of the apostles' meaning.

Neither the Scriptures, nor any subsequent history attest these sentiments; but supply circumstances, which render the opinion probable.

The Jews doubted the lawfulness of submission to the Roman yoke, and the christians being of the same nation, were apt, from the affinity of the two religions, to intermix the doctrines of both.

Again, as appears from St. Peter, some might understand the liberty, unto which they were called, as an emancipation from any authority merely human.

St. Paul has said, " Whoever resisteth the power, resisteth the ordinance of God."

This phrase, " the ordinance of God," cannot authorize any superstitious ideas of the regal character.

The expression is as applicable to one kind of government as another.

It is not affirmed of the supreme magistrate only, but of every inferior officer of the state.

The right of kings is the law of the land, and is ordained by God, only by virtue of that decree by which he sanctions every law of society, which promotes the general welfare.

According to the idea of the origin and constitution of princes, St. Peter denominates them, " the ordi-
" nance of man."

Of Civil Liberty. C. 5.

" Civil liberty is the not being restrained by any law,
" but what conduces in a greater degree to the public
" welfare."

To do what we will, is natural liberty; but this liberty can only exist in a state of solitude.

For in society the liberty of the individual would be checked by the opposition of other mens' wills.

Civil liberty is augmented by the very laws which restrain it:

Because the individual gains more by the limitation of other men's wills, than he suffers by the diminution of his own.

The above definition of liberty intimates,

1st. That restraint is an evil.

2d. That this evil ought to be overbalanced by some public advantage.

3d. That the proof of this advantage lies upon the legislature.

4th. That a law being found to produce no sensible good is a sufficient reason for repealing it.

This maxim might be remembered in a review of many laws in this country, especially,—

The game laws.

The poor laws.

The laws against papists and dissenters.

According to this account of civil liberty it follows,

That every nation possesses some, no nation perfect liberty.

That it is not to be totally lost or won by any one event or change whatever.

That the freedom or slavery of nations, or of the same nation at different times, is intelligible only in a comparative sense.

Hence the distinction between personal and civil liberty.

A citizen of the freest republic may be imprisoned, for his crimes:

But his civil liberty is not invaded, so long as his confinement is the effect of a beneficial public plan.

It is not the rigour, but the inexpediency of laws which makes them tyrannical.

Another common idea of civil liberty places it not merely in the exemption from noxious laws, but in the security from the danger of having any such hereafter.

Thus the late revolution deprived the Swedes of their liberty; though they are governed by the same or more just laws than before.

Thus the act of our parliament, which in the reign of Henry VIII. gave the king's proclamation the force of law, may be called a forfeiture of our liberty, though no proclamations were ever issued.

Thus a mild government under a despotic prince cannot be called civil liberty.

The various definitions which have been framed of civil liberty, all are adapted to the same idea; but labour under one inaccuracy, viz. They describe not so much liberty itself, as the various safeguards and preservatives of liberty.

Therefore those definitions ought to be rejected, which disturb the public content, by making that essential to our freedom; which is not attainable in experience.

Both ideas lead to this conclusion: that that people, government, and constitution, is the freest, which makes the best provision for the enacting of expedient and salutary laws.

Of different Forms of Government. C. 6.

In every government there necessarily exists a power, from which there is no appeal, and which is omnipotent.

The person or assembly, in whom this power resides, is called the sovereign power of the state.

Is called also the legislature of the state.

A government receives its denomination from the form of the legislature, which form is likewise what we mean by the constitution of a country.

There are three principal forms of government, from an intermixture of which all actual governments are composed.

1. Absolute monarchy.

2. An Aristocracy, the members of which fill up by election the vacancies of their own body, or succeed by inheritance, or some personal right.

3. A Republic.

The advantages of the first are unity of council, activity, and secrecy, military energy, exclusion of popular and aristocratical contention, and of the intrigues of ambition.

The mischiefs are tyranny, and its concomitant ignorance in the governors of the peoples' interest.

The advantage of aristocracy consists in the wisdom attained by experience and education.

The mischiefs are dissensions among the rulers, and partial laws to the oppression of the poor.

The advantages of a republic are, exemption from needless restrictions; equal laws, public spirit, frugality, averseness to war, the opportunity of calling forth the faculties of the best citizens.

The evils are, dissention, tumult, faction, the tyranny of the majority, the confusion and clamour of an assembled multitude, delay of public counsels, the intrigues of demagogues, &c.

Hence in a mixed government, which is composed of two or more simple forms, their separate advantages and evils are to be cultivated or provided against.

Sometimes a quality results from the conjunction of two simple forms of government which belongs not to the separate existence of either: thus corruption may spring up, where the supreme power is divided between an executive magistrate and a popular council.

An hereditary monarchy is preferable to an elective monarchy.

Experience has shewn this.

For the interests and passions of the electors exclude the consideration of the qualities of the competitors.

The assembly of the popular choice interrupts regular industry.

The king elected regards his opponents as enemies.

Plans of improvement are seldom brought to maturity, where the crown devolves by chance.

Aristocracies are of two kinds; first, where the power of the nobility belongs to them in their collective capacity alone.

This is the constitution of Venice.

2d. Where the nobles are severally invested with great personal power and immunities.

This is the constitution of Poland.

Of these two forms of government the first is more tolerable.

For however profligate each member may be in his private designs, not having the end to gain, they are not likely to unite in any specific act of oppression: or if they did, their power is confined: the tyranny does not extend to so many places at the same time, as it may be carried on by the dominion of a numerous nobility over their vassals.

Of all dominations this is the most odious.

The people of Europe have more than once deliberately exchanged it for the miseries of despotism.

E.G. Denmark in the middle of the last century.

The late revolution in Sweden owed its success to the same cause.

In England the depression of the barons under the house of Tudor.

G 2

The lesson from this is, that a mixed goverament which admits a patrician order ought jealously to circumscribe its privileges and immunities.

The following are by no means inconsiderable advantages in a democratic constitution, i. e. when the people partake of the legislature.

1st. The direction which it gives to the education and pursuits of the superior orders of the community, and consequently its important share in forming the public manners.

Ambition of political dignity will awaken respectable characters to the improvement of their intellectual faculties.

2. Popular election procures to the common people courtesy from their superiors, in whom it generates settled habits of condescension and respect.

3. The satisfaction which the people in free governments derive from the knowledge and agitation of political subjects;

A gratification by no means unimportant, for it supplies a substitute perhaps for drinking, gaming, scandal, and obscenity.

It has been a received opinion, that a republican form of government suits only a small state from the considerations :—

That unless the people in every district be admitted to a share in the national representation, the government is not, as to them, a republic.

That the elections are managed by the intrigues of a few.

That the interest of the constituent becomes too small ; of the representative too great :

The connection between them is difficult :

All appeal to the people is impossible from their numbers :

The factions and unanimity of the senate are equally dangerous :

The mechanism too complicated.

Much of this reason is done away by the contrivance of a federal republic, such as that of America.

It is yet to be tried :

To what limits it can safely enlarge its dominions ;

How far it is capable of uniting the liberty of a commonwealth with the safety of a powerful empire :

Whether dissensions will not arise from want of a common superior :

No record to judge by.

Of the British Constitution. C. 7.

By the *Constitution* of a country is meant so much of its law as relates to the designation and form of the legislature.

Therefore the terms constitutional and unconstitutional, mean legal and illegal.

In England the system of public jurisprudence is made up of acts of parliament, of decisions of courts of law, and of immemorial usage ;

Consequently these are the principles, of which the English constitution itself consists.

It is founded on no higher original, than that which gives force to the laws of the realm.

An act of parliament in England can never be properly called unconstitutional.

In a lower sense it may : viz. when it militates against the spirit of other salutary laws :

As when a parliament of Henry VIII. gave the King's proclamation the authority of law.

" Principles of the constitution," and other similar expressions often used, seem to refer to some distant æra, when the scheme of our government was formerly planned and settled.

No such plan was ever formed.

The constitution of England hath grown out of occasion and emergency.

Thus the Great Charter and the Bill of Rights were partial modifications of the constitution; they did not give it a new original.

In the British constitution there exists a wide difference between the actual state of government, and the theory; though the one results from the other.

Thus the king is invested with absolute personal impunity, with the power of conferring by charter the privilege of sending representatives into one house of parliament, and of placing whom he will in the other.

These prerogatives, which seem to make him despotic, are dwindled into mere ceremony.

In their stead has arisen a sure and commanding influence from the enormous patronage placed in the disposal of the executive magistrate.

Upon questions of reform, therefore, the change ought not to be adventured upon without a cool, sober, comprehensive discernment of the consequences.

For in politics the most important effects have for the most part been incidental and unforeseen; the direct consequences are often the least important.

Thus Elizabeth and her successor encouraged trade by wise laws.

They were not conscious, that at the same time they encouraged a consciousness of strength and independence, which could not long endure the dominion of arbitrary princes.

The mutiny act was made an annual bill merely from the expediency of retaining a controul over the most dangerous prerogative of the crown, the command of a standing army.

It has altered the whole frame of the British Constitution.

A standing army has become essential to the safety and administration of government.

Parliament by discontinuing this provision can enforce its resolutions on any subject.

A contest between the King and Parliament must dissolve the constitution.

Lastly, the nomination of all employments in the public service was conferred on the crown from the obvious propriety, that a master should choose his own servants: it has added an influence, which has changed the character of the constitution.

For patronage is power.

There is one end of civil government, peculiar to a good government; the happiness of its subjects.

There is another essential end, and common to it with many bad ones; its own preservation.

Many things in the English, as in every constitution, are to be vindicated solely as provisions for its permanency. They are, however, of subordinate consideration to the value of the constitution itself.

The Government of England is formed by a combination of the three regular species of government; the Monarchy, residing in the King; the Aristocracy, in the House of Lords; and the Republic, in the House of Commons.

Such a scheme is intended to unite the advantages of the several simple forms, and to exclude the inconveniences, as enumerated in the preceding chapter.

The subject may be considered by remarking the expedients, by which the British Constitution provides;

1st. For the interest of its subjects:

2d. For its own preservation.

The contrivances for the first are the following.

Every citizen is capable of becoming a member of the senate, and every senator has the right of propounding whatever law he pleases.

Every district has the privilege of choosing representatives informed of their interest.

The right of voting for representatives being annexed to different qualifications in different places, each order and profession of men in the community become virtually represented.

The elections are so connected with the influence of landed property, that a considerable number of men of great estates must be returned to parliament; and are also so modified, that men the most eminent in their profession are the most likely to prevail.

Their number, fortune, and various interests, and above all the temporary duration of their power, are securities for the freedom of their judgment.

The representatives are so mixed with their constituents, that they cannot impose a burthen, in which they do not themselves share.

The proceedings of parliament, and parliamentary conduct of each member, are known by the people at large.

Political importance depends so far upon public favour, that a member cannot more effectually raise himself to eminence, than by contriving salutary laws.

From all the above it may be presumed, that wise counsels will receive the approbation of the majority of the House of Commons.

For the advantage of monarchy the executive government is committed to an hereditary King.

In the defence of the empire; in the maintenance of its dignity; in the advancement of its trade by treaties; and in providing for the administration of municipal justice, the interest of the king and people usually coincides : in this part the regal office is therefore trusted with ample power.

In the articles of *taxation* and *punishment*, when their interests are different, the safety of the people is strictly guarded by the constitution.

Every law to levy money must originate in the House of Commons.

The application of the public supplies is watched, and is under certain regulation; the expenditure of them is accounted for in the House.

With respect to punishment, the guilt of the offender must be pronounced by twelve men of his own order; by a jury; and the punishment of each crime is fixed.

Illegal imprisoment is completly provided against by the *Habeas Corpus* act.

In a charge of treason where government is a party in the prosecution, the subject is assisted in his defence by extraordinary indulgencies: viz. A copy of his indictment, a list of the witnesses to be produced, and of the jury to be impannelled, ten days before trial: he is permitted to make his defence by counsel, and above all, two witnesses are required to convict him.

3d. The constitution provides for its own preservation, by what has been called the *ballance* of the constitution, which consists in two contrivances; a ballance of power, and a ballance of interest.

By the ballance of power, there is no power possessed by one part of the legislature, which it can abuse without being checked by the other.

If laws subversive of regal government are framed, the King can interpose his negative.

The parliament can check any arbitrary application of this negative by refusing supplies of money.

" The King can do no wrong:" but they who concur and assist in any illegal command, are subject to prosecution, and cannot plead his pardon.

No act of the crown can be legal, till authenticated by the subscription of some of its great officers.

The power of the crown over the military, and to declare war, can be checked by the Parliament's refusing supplies.

The influence of favoritism is subdued by the necessity of choosing men most capable of managing the state.

By the ballance of interest is meant this :—that the respective interests of the three estates are so adjusted, that whichever shall attempt any encroachment, the other two will unite in resisting it.

The proper use and design of the house of Lords is,

1st. To enable the King by his right of the peerage to reward the servants of the public at a small expence to the nation.

2d. To fortify the stability of the regal government.

3d. To stem the progress of popular fury.

Occasions may arise, in which the commonwealth may be saved by the reluctance of the nobility, who have separate prejudices and interests, to adopt the caprices, or to yield to the vehemence of the people.

If their privileges be restrained, there can be little inconvenience to the people from the increase of their number ;—the same quantity of power divided amongst more hands.

The admission of a small number of ecclesiastics into the house of Lords is an equitable compensation to the clergy, who are a body of considerable property, number, and influence, for their exclusion from the House of Commons.

If they should be obsequious, they are properly put in that house, where frequent resistance to Government is not expected.

No sufficient reason evident for exempting the persons of members of either House of Parliament from arrest for debt.

When extended to domestics and retainers, it becomes an absurd sacrifice of equal justice to imaginary dignity.

There is nothing in the British Constitution so remarkable, as the irregularity of the popular representation.

The House of Commons consists of 548 members, of whom 200 are elected by 700 constituents.

In one part of the kingdom a person may be one in twenty, who choose two representatives, in another he may have no representative at all.

It may be said, that one half of the House of Commons obtain their seats in that assembly by the election of the people, the other half by purchase, or by the nomination of the proprietors of great estates.

This incongruity in the constitution strikes most forcibly at first sight; but before we adventure upon reformation, we ought to be assured that the magnitude of the evil will justify the danger of the experiment.

We wave all controversy with those who wish to alter the *form* of the government; as the republican.

With those who insist upon representation as a *natural* right.

It is a natural right so far only as it conduces to the public utility, i. e. to the establishment of good laws, and as it secures to the people the just administration of them.

These effects depend on the abilities and dispositions of the national counsellors.

Wherefore if men most likely to know and promote the public interest are returned to parliament, it signifies little who return them.

H 2

In the house of Commons are found the most considerable landholders, and merchants of the kingdom; the heads of the army, navy, law; the occupiers of great offices in the state; together with many individuals eminent for their knowledge, eloquence, and activity.

Does any scheme of representation promise to collect together more wisdom, or to produce firmer integrity?

If we attend to effects, there is a just excuse for those points of the present representation, which appear at first view absurd.

No order or assembly of men whatever can long maintain their place and authority, of which the members do not individually possess a great share of personal importance.

The present arrangement secures a great weight of property to the house of Commons.

The constitution of the small borough contributes to this effect; as the appointment is generally annexed to certain great inheritances.

Elections purely popular are in this respect uncertain.

It has been observed, that conspicuous abilities are most frequently found with the representatives of small boroughs; this is natural.

They are most likely to become purchasers, who by their talents can make the best of the bargain.

The opulent patron, who gives a seat, finds his own interest consulted by the reputation and abilities of the person whom he nominates.

If certain of the nobility hold the appointment of some representative, it serves to maintain a beneficial alliance between the two branches of the legislature.

If a few boroughs lie at the disposal of the crown, whilst their number is known and small, they may be tolerated with little danger.

The present representatives, after all these deductions, are so connected with the mass of the community, that the will of the people, when determined and permanent, generally prevails.

The diminution of the influence of the crown is the chief design of the various schemes for a reform in parliament.

The more obvious and safe way of attaining the same end would be to reduce the patronage of the crown.

Many wise and virtuous politicians think it a necessary ingredient in the British constitution, which gives cohesion to the whole.

If the measures of government were opposed from nothing but principle, the government ought to have nothing but rectitude, to support them.

Faction, envy, a willingness to thwart ambition, love of shewing power, might induce a great party to draw to themselves the whole government, or wantonly and effectually to obstruct the business of the nation.

Government must possess an influence to counteract these motives; to produce, not a bias of the passions, but a neutrality.

Our own national history affords ground for these apprehensions.

Till the reign of Charles I. the king carried his measures by *intimidation*: after the restoration there succeeded, and has since the revolution been methodically pursued, the more successful expedient of influence.

The assemblies of the colonies in America possessed much of the constitution of our house of Commons.

The king had no influence among them.

To this cause, among others we may attribute the changes that have taken place.

These examples will have weight with those who consider stability among the first perfections of any government.

This apology for influence relates not to a justification of bribery, nor does it require any sacrifice of personal probity.

In political, above all other subjects, the wisest judgment may be held in suspence.

There are subjects of apparent indifference.

This occurs frequently in personal contests.

These cases compose the province of influence.

The only doubt is what influence shall be admitted.

If the influence of the crown is removed, another would succeed.

If motives of gratitude and expectation be withdrawn, others equally irrelevant to the merits of the question, will succeed in their place.

The success of influence in matters of indifference does not prove, that the consent of parliament could be procured to measures evidently detrimental.

There is more reason to fear, that without influence the prerogative could nor support itself.

From all the above we may conclude, that an independent parliament is incompatible with the existence of monarchy!

Of the administration of Justice.   C. 8.

The first maxim of a free state is that the laws be made by one set of men and administered by another, that the legislative and judicial authorities be kept separate :

Because then general laws are made by one body of men without seeing whom they may effect, and must be applied by the other, let them affect whom they will.

In this country the legislative and judicial functions are effectually divided.

This fundamental rule of civil jurisprudence is violated in cases of attainder or confiscation, in bills of pains and penalties, and in all *ex post facto* laws, in which parliament exercises the double office of legislature and judgment.

Experience has shewn, that in these instances the valuable rule had better never been infringed.

The escape of one delinquent cannot produce so much harm, as may arise from the infraction of a rule, on which the existence of civil liberty essentially depends.

The next security for the impartial administration of justice is the independence of the judges, especially in decisions to which government is a party.

The judges not unfrequently become arbiters between the king and people; they ought therefore to be independent of either.

This policy dictated that improvement in our constitution, by which the judges, though appointed by the king, can be removed by an address from both houses of parliament.

Their salaries ought to be such as may render their situation respectable, and desirable by men of eminence, and secure their integrity.

A third precaution to be observed in the formation of a court of judicature is, that the number of judges be small. For beside the violence and tumult inseparable from large assemblies, judges when they are numerous, divide the shame of an unjust determination; whereas each should be responsible in his separate and particular reputation. This has been exemplified in the transferring of the trial of parliamentary elections from the house of Commons to a select committee.

An even number of judges, is preferable to an odd one, and four seems better than any other, as there must be a majority of three to one.

A fourth requisite in the constitution of a court of justice is, that it be held *apertis foribus.*

Something is gained to the public by appointing two or three courts of concurrent jurisdiction, that it may be in the option of the suitor, to which he will resort.

But lastly, one supreme tribunal is necessary, by whose final sentence all other courts should be bound.

This preserves an uniformity in the decisions of inferior courts, and maintains to each its proper limits.

There are two kinds of judicature, the one, where the office of judge is permanent in the same person; the other, where the judge is determined by lot at the time of trial.

The advantage of the former is the knowledge and readiness of experience: the defect, the possibility (as he is known before hand) of secret management.

The advantage of the latter is indifferency: the defect, the want of legal science, which may produce uniformity.

The construction of English courts of law in which causes are tried by the jury with the assistance of a judge, combines both the two with peculiar success.

Every deviation from this mode of trial, such as summary convictions before justices of the peace, and courts of conscience, ought to be watched with vigilance.

The trial by jury is sometimes inadequate to the administration of equal justice.

This takes place chiefly in disputes in which some popular passion intervenes; as

Where an order of men are obnoxious from their profession, as are officers of the revenue, &c. or where the interest of one of the party may be in common with the general interests of the jurors, as in contests between landlords and tenants, &c.

Or, lastly; where the minds are inflamed by political or religious dissensions.

Causes of this kind might be better removed from the neighbourhood of the parties.

The experiment of leaving it to the judges only is too big with public danger.

The situation of the courts of judicature presents an alternative of difficulties.

If there were only a few courts, and those in the metropolis, the consequence would be great expence in the conveyance to it, and prolixity of proceeding.

If domestic tribunals be erected in each neighbourhood, there is danger of ignorance and partiality in the judge of the supreme tribunal.

Our itinerary courts are relieved from both these objections, and there becomes one law of the land in every part of the kingdom.

Next to the constitution of courts of justice, the maxims which ought to guide them, are to be considered.

The chief point of enquiry here is, how far, and for what reasons, or whether at all, it is expedient to adhere to precedents; or whether it be necessary for judges to attend to any other consideration, than the apparent and particular equity of the case before them.

Precedents ought not to be incontrovertible, because this would give the sentence of judges all the authority which we ascribe to the most solemn acts of the legislature: yet the general security requires, that such precedents should not be overthrown without the detection of manifest error.

1. That the discretion of judges may be bound by a positive rule.

2. And principally, that the subject, where his legal interest is concerned, may know beforehand, how to act and what to expect.

The superintendency of parliament could not con-
s

trous abuses of judicial discretion, if there was no acknowledged standard of what is right.)

Without this knowledge the spirit of litigation must prevail, and the worst property of slavery would be entailed on the subject, no assurance of his rights, or knowledge of his duty.

However, from adherence to precedents, two inconveniencies arise :—

The hardship of particular determination, and the intricacy of the law, as a science.

To the first we may answer, that uniformity is of more importance than equity, in proportion as general uncertainty would be a greater evil than particular injustice.

The second is attended with no greater inconvenience, than that of erecting the law into a separate profession.

To a thinking mind this question frequently occurs ; —Why, since the maxims of natural justice are few and evident, do there arise so many doubts and controversies in their application? If a system of morality, containing both the precepts of revelation, and deductions of reason may be comprised in one moderate volume, what need of those tomes of statutes and reports?

In answer to this it is to be observed :

1. That treatises of morality always suppose facts to be ascertained, and the intention likewise of the parties to be laid open.

The discussion of these facts and the discovery of these intentions remain to exercise the enquiry of courts of justice, wherein the arbitration must proceed upon rules of evidence and maxims of credibility, with which the morality has no concern.

2. There exist a number of cases in which the law of nature prescribes nothing except that some certain rule

be adhered to, which has been introduced by an act of the legislature, or by custom.

Thus in the descent of lands, &c. from intestate proprietors, whether the kindred of the grandmother, or great grandmother, shall be preferred in the succession; whether sons shall be preferred to daughters, or the elder to the younger, and in various other questions which relate to the right or acquisition of property.

Many things are in their nature *indeterminate*, as the age of legal discretion.

Other things are perfectly arbitrary, as the time which should be assigned and limited for defendants to plead to the complaints alledged against them, and almost all those rules which constitute what is called the practice of the court.

3. In contracts between merchant, servant, &c. whether expressed or implied, which involve a great number of conditions, natural justice can only refer to the custom of the country.

4. As the laws of nature require, that the just engagements which a man enters into, should continue in force beyond his own life, the private rights of persons frequently depend upon what has been transacted in times remote from the present.

Thus in questions between lords of manors and their tenants; the king, and those who claim royal franchises; in tracing boundaries, &c. old covenants must be referred to, concerning the existence or conditions of which doubts must perpetually occur.

5. The quantity or extent of an injury is often dubious and undefined, and cannot be ascertained by any rule which the law of nature supplies; as when a man may have suffered in his person by any assault, or in the comfort of his life by the seduction of his wife or daughter, &c.

6. Controversies arise in the interpretations of written laws, originating in some contingency which the composer of the law did not foresee.

7. In the deliberations of courts of justice on every new question, a difficulty arises between the attention which is due to the truth and justice of the cause between the parties, and to the consequences of the principle which the precedent establishes.

Finally; one principal source of disputation must be *" the competition of opposite analogies."*

Questions arise continually, which resemble others where the point of law is fixed, only in part.

It is in the reconciliation of different analogies, that the contention of the bar is carried on : as in the dispute concerning literary and other property.

The few questions referred to superior courts shew, that doubtful and obscure points of law are not so numerous as they are apprehended to be.

There are two peculiarities in the judicial constitution of this country, which do not carry with them that evidence of their propriety, which recommends every other part of the system.

1. The rule, which requires that juries should be *unanimous* in their verdict.

To expect that twelve men promiscuously taken should be unanimous on a point confessedly dubious is absurd.

The effects are not so detrimental as the rule is unreasonable.

For in criminal prosecutions it operates on the side of mercy : in civil cases it adds weight to the direction of the judge, as the jury will naturally close their disputes by a subscription to the opinion of the bench.

However, there would be more assurance that the conclusion is founded in reasons of apparent truth and justice, if it were left to a certain majority.

2. The choice of the house of Lords, as the last and highest court of appeal.

There is nothing in the constitution of that assembly that should qualify them for this ardous office, except that the elevation of their rank and fortune affords a security against the influence of bribes.

The effect has proved the truth of this maxim, "That when a single institution is extremely dissonant from other parts of the system to which it belongs, it will always find some way of reconciling itself to the analogy which governs and pervades the rest."

By constantly placing in the house of Lords some of the most eminent lawyers, and by the undisputed deference which the members pay to the learning of their colleagues, the judges; the appeal is in fact made to the collected wisdom of our supreme courts of justice.

These, however, even if real, are minute imperfections.

The equal administration of the laws is the first blessing of social union, and we enjoy this blessing in perfection above any other nation.

Of Crimes and Punishments. C. 9.

The proper end of human punishment is not the satisfaction of justice, but the prevention of crimes.

By the satisfaction of justice is meant the retribution of so much pain for so much guilt; which is the dispensation we expect at the hand of God.

Now that, which is the cause and end of punishment, ought to regulate the measure of its severity.

Hence crimes are not by any government punished in proportion to their guilt, nor in all cases ought to be so, but in proportion to the difficulty and necessity of preventing them.

Thus the law denounces a severer punishment against stealing goods out of a shop, than out of a house,

It follows that punishments ought not to be rendered severe, when the crime can be prevented by any other means.

Thus since the practice of weighing gold, the sanguinary laws against counterfeiting or dimishing the gold coin have slept.

A breach of trust is a greater crime than other frauds, but is punished with less severity, because it may be prevented by proper circumspection in the choice of persons, &c. &c.

Where the confidence is unavoidable, as in a servant, &c. the sentence of the law is not less severe, and is more rigorously executed, then if no trust had intervened.

In pursuance of the same principle, the facility with which any species of crime is perpetrated, is deemed a reason for aggravating the punishment.

Thus of this kind are sheep-stealing, the stealing of cloth from tenters, &c.

From the justice of an omniscient God, we may expect a gradation of punishment proportioned to the guilt abstracted from any foreign consideration.

This cannot be expected from the government of man, whose authority over his fellow creatures is limited by defects of power and knowledge.

There are two methods of adminisering penal justice.

The first method assigns capital punishments to few offences, and inflicts it invariably.

The second assigns it to many kinds of offences, but inflicts only upon a few examples of each kind.

The latter method has been long adopted in this country.

The preference of this to the former method is founded on the consideration, that the selection of proper objects for capital punishments depends on circumstances, which cannot be ascertained with that exactness which is requisite in legal description.

Hence although it be necessary, that the whole authority of the legislature should fix by precise rules the limit to which punishment may be extended, yet the mitigation of punishment may be entrusted without danger to the executive magistrate, whose discretion will operate on the circumstances.

If judgment of death were reserved for a few species of crimes only, many crimes of dangerous example would go unpunished.

If there were no power of relaxation, some would undergo this punishment, when it was neither deserved, nor necessary.

By the latter expedient used in England few actually suffer death, while the dread and danger of it hangs over many.

The wisdom of this mode excuses the multiplicity of capital offences in the English code.

Privately stealing from the persons is a crime, the making of which capital, can hardly be defended on the abovementioned principles.

For it excludes every degree of force, and might be prevented by common circumspection.

The prerogative of pardon is properly reserved to the chief magistrate.

It is too high a power for many hands, or for any inferior officer in the state.

The king can best collect advice, and is removed at the greatest distance from private motives.

The exercise of this power is as much a judicial act as the trial of the prisoner.

Consequently any partiality in the exercise of it is as heinous as corruption in a judge.

Aggravations, which ought to guide the magistrate in the selection of objects for condign punishment, are principally these three: repetition; cruelty; combination.

In crimes perpetrated by a multitude, it is proper to separate in the punishment the ringleader from his followers.

This casts an obstacle in the way of such confederacies.

Injuries effected by terror and violence ought chiefly to be repressed; because their extent is unlimited: because no private precaution can protect the subject against them: because they endanger life and safety, as well as property: because they render the condition of society wretched by a sense of personal insecurity.

These reasons do not apply to fraud, which circumspection can prevent, &c.

In estimating the comparative malignancy of crimes of violence, regard is to be had not only to the mischief of the crime, but the fright occasioned by the attack.

This consideration places a difference between breaking into a dwelling house by day and by night: this difference obtains in the punishment of the offence by the law of Moses, and in the codes of most countries.

Of injuries which are effected without force, the most noxious are forgeries, counterfeiting or diminishing the coin, and the stealing of letters in the course of their conveyance.

Though these seem to affect property alone, yet their general consequences, if they became frequent, would tend to lay waste human existence.

They who regard the divine rule of life for life, and blood for blood, may perceive with respect to the effects of action a great resemblance between certain atrocious frauds, and those crimes which attack personal safety.

There appears a substantial difference between the forging of bill of exchange, &c. where credit is given merely the signature, and between the forging of bonds, &c. where deceit might be precluded by proper circumspection in the parties.

The law however makes no difference.

Perjury is a crime, the general consequences of which might be put on a level with the most flagitious fraud.

The obtaining of money by secret threats deserves to be reckoned among the worst species of robbery.

The frequency of capital executions in this country owes its necessity to three causes; much liberty, great cities, and the want of punishment short of death possessing a sufficient degree of terror.

With respect to the first, the jealousies with which a free people watch their liberties, will not permit the controul, which is exercised with success in arbitrary governments, such as the master of a family rendering an account of all his inmates, the patrol of soldiers in the streets, &c.

With respect to the second, great cities present easier opportunities and incentives to libertinism, enable them to collect in confederacy, afford concealment, &c.

3. Transportation which is the sentence second in the order of severity, answers the purpose of example very imperfectly.

Because it is a slight punishment to those who have no home.

Because the punishment is unobserved and unknown.

This chasm in the scale of punishment produces two great imperfections.

1. It extends the same punishment to crimes of different magnitude.

K

2. Punishments separated by a wide interval are assigned to crimes hardly distinguished in their guilt.

The end of punishment is twofold, *amendment* and *example*.

In the first little has been effected, criminals generally returning more hardened.

Pardons at the point of death might now and then have great effect, but cannot be often repeated.

Of the reforming punishments, *solitary* imprisonment promises the most success.

As aversion to labour is the cause from which half the vices of low life proceed, punishments should be contrived with a view to the conquering of this disposition.

A portion of the prisoner's earnings by labour should be left to his use, and confinement might be measured by quantity of work.

The principal question is, what to do with criminals after enlargement.

It is worth the attention of all, who wish well to the country, to consider what means will best answer the two great purposes of employment and dispersion.

Torture is applied to extort confessions of guilt, or to prolong the pains of death.

The question by torture is equivocal in its effects, pain operating in like manner upon the innocent and guilty.

False accusations may be extracted from the one, truth from the other.

Barbarous spectacles tend either to harden and deprave the public feelings, or sink mens' abhorrence of the crime in their commiseration of the criminal.

That mode of punishment is preferable which augments the horror of the punishment without impairing the public sensibility.

Infamous punishments are to be confined to offences universally detested, and to offenders sensible of shame.

The certainty of punishment is of more consequence than the severity.

Criminals encourage themselves more with the chance of escape, than compare the fruits of their crime with the probable pain of punishment.

Those contrivances directed towards the restraint of crimes are most effectual, which facilitate the conviction of criminals.

Upon this principle, the scrupulousness of juries in demanding proofs of a crime, of which its nature and secresy scarcely admit, is injurious to society.

It encourages villany by confessing the impossibility of bringing villains to justice.

Two maxims are generally the cause of these injudicious acquittals.

1st. " That circumstantial evidence falls short of positive proof."

This is untrue; a concurrence of well authenticated circumstances being a stronger ground of assurance than positive testimony unconfirmed by circumstances.

2d. " That it is better for ten guilty to escape, than for one innocent to suffer."

But the security of civil life being protected by the dread of punishment, the misfortune of an individual cannot be put in competition with this object.

Though every care should be taken of each individual, yet courts of justice ought not to be deterred by every appearance of danger.

Of Religious Establishments, and of Toleration. C. 10.

A religious establishment is no part of christianity; it is only the means of inculcating it.

No commands were delivered by Christ for establishing any form of church government, with a view of fix-

K 2

ing a constitution for succeeding ages, to be adopted every where, and at all times by christians.

This reserve is sufficiently accounted for by two reasons.

1st. That no precise constitution could be framed, adapted equally to the church in its primitive state, with the condition it was to assume, when become a national religion.

2dly. That a particular designation of offices among his primitive ministers might, by interfering with the civil policy, have obstructed the progress of the religion itself.

The authority therefore of a church establishment is founded upon its utility, " as a scheme of instruction."

The notion of a religious establishment comprehends three things.

1st. A clergy.

2d. A legal provision for their maintenance.

3d. Confining that provision to the teachers of a particular sect of christianity.

In defending ecclesiastical establishments, the first and fundamental question is,—Whether christianity can be maintained, unless a class of men be set apart from other employments by public authority, to the study and teaching of religion, and the conducting of public worship?

A clergy is necessary, because it is an historical religion, and requires a peculiar and very comprehensive branch of knowledge, the dead languages, Jewish history, &c. and because the ordinary office of public teaching requires qualifications not usually to be met with amidst the offices of civil life.

To obtain these qualifications, study, preparation, leisure, and a peculiar education are necessary.

2d. Whether their maintenance should depend on the will of their hearers, or be assigned by law?

To the scheme of voluntary contributions there are the following objections:

That they depend on caprice, therefore no permanent maintenance.

That people might be tempted to prefer their interest to religion.

That the ministry would be degraded by the idea of begging.

3d. Whether this provision shall be confined to one sect in preference to all others of irreconcilable opinions?

This question is dependent on another, viz. How and by whom shall ministers be appointed?

If our species of patronage be retained, a test is necessary to prevent discordancy of opinions between the teacher and congregation.

If the appointment be in the hands of the separate parishes, there would be endless disputes among the different sects about the choice of the minister.

If it be in the state, a national religion commences immediately.

The legal maintenance of a clergy, without a legal preference of one sect to another, seems practicable only in a mode said to have been adopted in North America.

Every man is obliged to contribute towards the maintenance of religion, but the choice of the sect, to whose ministers he contributes, is left to himself.

To this mode are the following inconveniences:

1st. That it is incompatible with the first requisite of an ecclesiastical establishment, the division of the country into parishes of a commodious extent.

2d. That strifes and an interested spirit of proselytism would arise, where the pecuniary success of the different ministers is made to depend on the number and wealth of their followers.

Of a national religion a test is the immediate and indispensable consequence.

Tests are liable to be unjustifiably extended, multiplied and continued.

They check inquiry, violate liberty, ensnare the consciences of the clergy by tempting them to prevaricate, and from the changes in mens opinions in religion, come at length to contradict the actual sentiments of the church.

If the division of the country into districts, with a minister to each, in which all churches agree, be a substantial part of a religious establishment, the question occurs,—Whether equality or distinction of orders among the clergy, conduces most to the ends of the institution.

In favour of our system are the following reasons:

That it secures peace and subordination among the clergy.

That it provides for each rank in civil life its corresponding minister;

That it is an allurement to men of talents to enter into the church, and a stimulus to the industry of those who are in it.

A national religion being established, how shall dissenters be treated?

This question is preceded by another,—Whether the civil magistrate is justified in interfering in religious matters at all.

They who deduce civil government from some stipulation with its subjects, contend, that religion was excepted out of the social compact, and that in an affair between God and a man's own conscience, no authority could be transferred from the latter to another.

We, however, who derive it from the will of God, *allow the magistrate to interfere in every matter civil and religious, as far as it conduces in its general tendency to the common good.*

But religion pertaining to the interests of a life to come lies beyond the province of civil government.

Laws, when they interfere even in religion, interfere only with temporals.

My salvation is out of the power of man to effect, but even my life may be taken away on account of my religion, because it may be taken away from any man for any reason that the legislature may deem conducive to the general good.

As religion too can be construed to extend to all offices of life, its exemption from the control of laws might afford a plea to exclude civil government from all authority over the subject.

Still it is right " to obey God rather than man."

In religious matters the right of the magistrate to ordain, and the obligation of the subject to obey, may be very different.

This difference seldom happens in civil affairs.

The law authorizes what it enjoins.

But when laws, by exacting particular modes of worship and tenets of faith, contradict what a man thinks has been declared by God to be true, whatever plea the state has to justify its edict, the subject has none to excuse his compliance.

The conclusion from the above proposition may be, that as to promote the salvation of men is to promote public happiness, the supreme magistrate may and ought to enforce in any manner that religion, which he thinks most acceptable to God.

But the clause in the above proposition, " general tendency," obliges the magistrate to reflect,

1st. Whether the religion he wishes to propagate, be best calculated to secure the eternal welfare of the subject.

2d. Whether the means he employs will establish that religion.

3d. What will be the consequences of a general adoption of this interference?

What degree then, and sort of interference of secular laws in religious matters will most benefit public happiness?

Our conclusion upon this head will be regulated by two maxims:

1st. That any form of christianity is better than no religion.

2d. That the system of faith is best which is truest.

From the first it follows, that when the laws establish a national religion, they exercise a power and interference, which in their general tendency may benefit mankind.

But which religion shall the magistrate establish, his own, or that which generally prevails?

Assuming it to be an equal chance, whether of the two religions contains most truth, the latter should be established, if to teach the people their own religion be easier and better, than to convert them to another.

Upon these principles we must determine the case of dissenters.

Toleration as far as it regards liberty of conscience, and secures men in the possession of their religion, is expedient, and their right, as it conduces to the propagation of truth.

The confining a subject to the state religion is a needless and grievous violation of natural liberty.

Persecution never convinces, but forces men to prevaricate, and disgraces christianity.

Serious books should be tolerated, but the circulation of ridicule and invective upon religious subjects may justly be restrained.

Of complete toleration, that is, of admitting dissenters into offices and employments, doubts have been entertained;

For their opinions may be incompatible with the necessary functions of civil government, and therefore justify their exclusion from employments.

Even *discordancies* of religion, that not at all affect government, may render men unfit to act together in public stations.

This assertion is altogether unfounded; indeed there are no tenets in the religion of the several sects, that actually prevail, the quakers excepted, which incapacitate men for the service of the state.

In two cases the test laws are applied, and may be defended.

1st. Where two religions are contending for establishment, for one must have a decided superiority, in order to put an end to the contest.

2d. Where some disaffection towards the subsisting government is connected with certain religious distinctions.

The test is justifiable here upon the principle of interest; though it is not to the religion that the laws object, but to the religion as a mark of disaffection.

But why does not the legislature direct his test against the political principles, rather than encounter them through the medium of religious tenets?

To this there are two answers.

1st. The laws fear not opinions, but inclinations; and political inclinations can certainly be detected only by

L

the discovery of the religious creed with which they are wont to be connected.

2d. That when men renounce their religion, they commonly quit all connexion with the members of the church they have left.

The result of all is this :—" That a comprehensive na-
" tional religion, guarded by a few articles of peace and
" conformity, together with a legal provision for the
" clergy of that religion, and with a complete tolera-
" tion of dissenters, without any other exception than
" what arises from the conjunction of dangerous politi-
" cal dispositions with certain religious tenets, appears
" to be not only the most just and liberal, but the wisest
" and safest system, which a state can adopt.

Of Population and Provision ; and of Agriculture and Commerce, as subservient thereto. C. 11.

The final view of all rational politics is to produce the greatest quantity of happiness in a country.

The riches, strength, and glory of nations have no farther value, than as they contribute to this end.

2d. Though we speak of communities as of *sentient beings*, nothing really exists or feels but *individuals*.

Notwithstanding the diversity of conditions and extreme cases of slavery, the collective happiness of the inhabitants of any district will be nearly in the proportion of their numbers.

A larger portion of happiness is enjoyed by *ten* persons possessing the means of healthy subsistence, than can be produced by *five*, with every advantage of affluence and luxury.

Hence it follows, that the improvement of population is an object which ought to be preferred to *every other* political purpose.

A competition can seldom arise between the advancement of population, and any measure of real utility, as whatever tends to make a people happier, tends also to render them more numerous.

Various indications demonstrate the tendency of nature in the human species, to a continual increase of numbers.

What causes confine or check the natural progress of this multiplication?

Evidently the population of a country must stop, when the inhabitants are already so numerous, as to exhaust all the provision which the soil can produce.

But in the most cultivated regions, the number of marriageable women, who remain in each country unmarried, and the quantity of waste or mismanaged surface, shew how much both the numbers of the inhabitants, and the productions of the earth, may be augmented.

Even in our own country, however highly it be cultivated, the quantity of human provision might be increased five-fold.

The fundamental proposition on the subject of population is this :—" Wherever the commerce between the " sexes is regulated by marriage, and a provision for " that mode of subsistence, to which each class of the " community is accustomed, can be procured with ease " and certainty, there the number of people will in- " crease, and the rapidity, as well as the extent, of the " increase, will be proportioned to the degree in which " these causes exist."

This proposition contains several principles.

1st. " The necessity of confining the intercourse of " the sexes to the marriage union." Because,

It is only in the marriage union, that this intercourse is sufficiently prolific.

Family establishments alone are fitted to secure a succession of generations.

Nature has provided a stimulus sufficient to assure the frequency of marriages, while the male sex are prohibited from irregular gratifications:

Therefore, whenever subsistence is become scarce, it behoves the state to watch over the public morals with increased solicitude.

2d. It states as necessary to the success of population, " the ease and certainty with which a provision can be " procured for that mode of subsistence, to which each " class of the community is accustomed."

It is not the ease and certainty of procuring subsistence merely, but of that kind of subsistence which custom has established in each country.

At present, habitual superfluities in every station of life are become actual wants, and men will not marry, when by so doing they are to reduce their wants to the mere sustenance of nature.

Three causes worthy of distinct consideration regulate this point, upon which the state and progress of population depend.

1. The mode of living which actually obtains in a country.

China, where fish forms the principal food, and is very easily procured; and Hindostan, where nothing is eaten but rice, which is profusely plentiful, (and in warm climates food is the only necessary of life) are populous, notwithstanding the injuries of a despotic and unsettled government;—but should any revolution of manners introduce a taste for flesh, it would soon become a necessary of life, and from this change alone the population would soon suffer a great diminution.

Hence may be understood the true evil of luxury.

As it supplies employment, and promotes industry, it assists population:

But when by rendering the accommodations of life more artificial, it encreases the difficulty of maintaining a family, the effect of it is, that marriages are less frequent.

Luxury, therefore, considered with a view to population, acts by two opposite effects, and it is probable, that there exists a point to which luxury may ascend with advantage to the community, and beyond which it begins to be prejudicial.

Though this point depends on circumstances too intricate to admit of a precise solution, the following general rules may be established.

1. Of different kinds of luxury those are most innocent which afford employment to the greatest number of artists, &c.

2d. It is the diffusion rather than the degree of luxury which is to be dreaded as a national evil.

As the mischief of luxury is its obstructing marriage while it is confined to the few, the rich, much of the benefit and little of the evil is felt; but when it descends into the mass of the people, it checks the formation of families in an alarming degree.

3d. That the condition most favourable to population is that of a laborious frugal people administering to the demands of an opulent luxurious nation.

II. Next to the mode of living, we are to consider " the quantity of provision suited to that mode, which " is either raised in the country, or imported into it."

The extent and quality of soil being given, the quantity of provision varies according to its kind.

Tillage is universally preferable to pasturage, as the kind of provision which it produces goes much farther in the sustentation of human life.

It also affords employment to much greater numbers.

The *kind* and *quality* of provision, together with the extent and capacity of the soil being the same, the *quantity* will vary according to the *ability* of the occupier, and the *encouragement* he receives.

The greatest misfortune of a country is an indigent tenantry; this evil is felt, where agriculture is accounted a servile employment; where farms are extremely subdivided; where leases are unknown, or are of short or precarious duration.

A small capital cramps every operation of husbandry. The true *encouragement* of husbandry is the securing to the *occupier*, (i. e. he who procures the labour, and directs the management, whether tenant or proprietor) an exclusive right to the produce, so that the advantage of every improvement go to the improver.

Hence the objection to the holding of lands by the state, the king, corporate bodies, &c. as such proprietors seldom contribute much either of attention or expence to the estate, yet claim, by the rent, a part of the profit of every improvement upon it.

This complaint can only be obviated by " long leases at a fixed rent."

III. The *distribution* of provision becomes of equal consequence with the production, because the plenty of provision only benefits population, according as it is *distributed.*

The principle of " exchange" is the only universal principle of distribution.

The only equivalents to be offered in exchange are *power* and *labour.*

All property is *power,* and money is the representative of power; this is necessarily confined to a few, and is soon exhausted : but *labour* is a constant fund, and in every man's possession.

Employment must therefore be the medium of distribution, and thus it affects population " directly."

(It is erroneous to consider the production and the distribution as independent of each other.

The quantity produced will evidently be regulated by the demand on sale, which alone excites the diligence of the husbandman : but the demand depends on the number of those who can return in exchange other fruits of industry.)

It affects population " indirectly," as it augments the stock of provision, by furnishing purchasers.

On this basis, its subserviency to population is founded the public benefit of trade and foreign commerce.

We acknowledge the benefit of those few trades, and that small portion of commerce, which supply the immediate wants of life, as food and clothing, &c. but of more than half our trade, and almost all our commerce, it may be asked,—

" How, since they add nothing to the stock of provi-
" sions do they tend to increase the number of the
" people ?"

The answer is contained in the discussion of another question :— " Since the soil will maintain many more
" than it can employ, what must be done, supposing
" the country to be full, with the remainder of the in-
" habitants ?"

They who have a right to the produce of the soil either by the rule of partition or their labour, will not part with their property for nothing, or rather will not raise more than they themselves want, or can exchange for what they want.

Or if they were willing, still the most enormous mischiefs would ensue from so many remaining unemployed.

This part, therefore, find employment in fabricating

or procuring, what may gratify or requite those, who possess the produce of the soil.

A certain portion only of human labour can be productive, the rest is instrumental—both are equally necessary, nor does it signify, how superfluous the articles may be, which are furnished by trade, or procured by commerce.

Let it be remembered, then, that agriculture is the immediate source of human provision, that trade conduces to the production of provision, only as it promotes agriculture; that the whole system of commerce has no other public importance than its subserviency to this end.

To return: "employment universally promotes population."

Hence it follows, that every branch of commerce is of public importance in proportion to the numbers, to which it furnishes materials for industry.

The first place belongs to the exchange of wrought goods for raw materials.

The second place is due to that commerce which barters one wrought article for others.

The last and lowest species is the exportation of raw materials for wrought goods.

This trade is unfavourable to population, as it causes no demand for employment, either in what it takes out of the country, or what it brings into it.

Of different branches of *manufactory* those are most beneficial, in which the price of the wrought article exceeds in the greatest proportion that of the raw materials.

The produce of the ground is never the most advantageous article of foreign commerce: under a perfect state of public œconomy, the soil of the country should be applied solely to the raising of provision for the inhabitants, and its trade be supplied by their industry.

We have hitherto considered the inhabitants of a country as supported by the produce of the country: but where the provision is imported, the reasoning will apply to the article, which is exchanged for provision, whether it be money, produce, or labour.

Thus the Dutch raise madder, and exchange it for corn: and earn money to procure the provision which their own country cannot supply, by carrying the produce of one country to another.

The increase or decline of this carrying trade would affect population in that country no less, than similar changes in the cultivation of the soil.

These few principles will enable us to describe, what effects upon population may be expected from the following important articles of national conduct and œconomy.

I. Emigration—may either be the overflowing of a country, or the desertion. When a country is overstocked with inhabitants, emigration neither indicates any political decay, nor in truth diminishes the people, nor ought to be discouraged.

Where emigrants quit their country from insecurity, oppression, &c. it would be in vain to keep them at home, as these same causes would prevent their multiplication if they remained.

The laws can effectually interfere with those only who emigrate from the allurement of climate, nominal higher wages &c. But from the attachment to home, this class will always be but small.

II. Colonization.—We can only consider it in its tendency to promote population in the parent state.

Colonists naturally apply themselves to the cultivation of the soil: in exchange for the produce they receive the manufactures of the mother country, which

M

thus feels an increase both of employment and provision.

Thus it promotes the two grand requisites on which depends the state of population; distribution, and provision.

When the colony does not remit provision, still the exportation of wrought goods, in whatever articles they are paid for, advances population in that secondary way.

III. Money.—Where it abounds the people are generally numerous: for population is promoted by employment; of which money is partly the indication, and partly the cause.

Money *flows into* a country in return for its exports, and is *retained in* a country, by the country supplying in a great measure its own manufactures.

Still employment, not money is the cause of population, for money may be plentiful, where the country is poor and ill-peopled, as Spain.

But, secondly, money may be an operative cause of population, by stimulating industry, and facilitating the means of subsistence, neither of which depends on the price of labour, or of provision, but on the proportion they bear to each other, which proportion is advanced by the influx of money.

It is not the quantity but the constant increase of that quantity of money, from which this advantage arises.

IV. Taxation.—Taxes are not necessarily prejudicial to population, as they take nothing out of a country.

The effect of taxes upon the means of subsistence depends not so much on the amount of the sum levied, as upon the object and application of the tax.

Nevertheless in a great plurality of instances their tendency is noxious: the people must either contract their wants, and thus diminish consumption and employment, or by raising the price of labour, check the sale of their productions and manufacture at foreign markets, even when taxes are levied on *proper objects* and for *proper purposes*.

Abuses are inseparable from the disposal of public money : as governments are usually administered, the produce of public taxes is expended upon a train of gentry, in the maintaining of pomp, or in the purchase of influence.

A wise statesman will adjust his taxes so as to give the least possible obstruction to the means of subsistence of the mass of the people.

A tax, to be just, ought to rise upon the different classes of the community in a much higher ratio, than the simple proportion of their incomes :

For it ought to regard not what men have, but what they can spare.

A due proportion can only be preserved by a system and variety of taxes, mutually balancing and equalizing one another.

V. Exportation of bread-corn.——Nothing seems more injurious to population than this; yet this has been the policy of the wisest legislators :

For " it is impossible to have enough without a superfluity."

If the crop be adequate to the consumption of a year of scarcity, it must exceed the consumption in a year of plenty, and the exportation of the occasional redundancy does not lessen the number maintained by the produce of the soil.

Here the benefits of foreign commerce belong to this in common with other species of trade : beside the encouragement which the prospect of sale at a competent price affords to the industry of the husbandman.

Likewise in a newly-settled country, corn may not

only form an export, but the people can thrive by no other means.

Except in these two cases exportation of bread-corn is always noxious.

VI. Abridgement of labour does not injure population.

In proportion as each article can be afforded at a lower price, from an easier or shorter process in the manufacture, it will either grow into more general use, or an improvement will take place in the quality and fabric which will demand a proportionable addition of hands.

From this reasoning we may judge how far laws can contribute to population. On the dissoluteness of manners, on men's mode of living and their artificial wants, which are the impediments to marriage, laws can have little effect.

By their protection, they may promote industry, but without industry they can provide neither subsistence nor employment.

All attempts to *force trade* by laws will be evaded; their interference in trade is salutary only when they are intended to prevent frauds.

The chief advantage to population from the interference of law, consists in the encouragement of agriculture.

For this purpose, the laws of property should be adjusted to the following rules:

1st. " To give to the occupier all the power over the " soil which is necessary to its perfect cultivation.

2d. " To assign the whole profit of every improvement " to the person by whom it is carried on."

It is of little consequence in whose hands or to what extent land is, if it be rightly used.

There exists in this country conditions of tenure which condemn the land to perpetual sterility.

The *right of common* precludes each proprietor from improving his estate, without the consent of many others.

This is also usually embarrassed by *manerial* claims.

But, secondly, agriculture is discouraged by every constitution of landed property, which admits to a participation of the profit, those who have no concern in the improvement. This objection is applicable to all such customs of manors, as subject the proprietor upon the death of the lord or tenant or the alienation of the estate, to a fine apportioned to the improved value of the land.

But of all institutions none is so noxious as that of tithes; these are a tax upon industry, and upon that precise mode of cultivation, which it is the *business of the state* to relieve and remunerate.

No measure of so great concern is so easy and beneficial as that of converting tithes into corn-rents, which would secure to the tithe holder an equivalent for his interest, and leave to industry its entire reward.

Of War, and of Military Establishments.

Though the Christian scriptures describe wars as crimes or judgments, the profession of a soldier is no where forbidden or condemned.

It is difficult to apply the principles of morality to the affairs of nations, because the " particular conse-" quence sometimes appears to exceed the value of the " general rule."

For instance, an adherence to a public treaty might enslave a whole people, &c.

Yet if the rules of relative justice are to be violated in these cases; if treaties are no longer binding than whilst they are convenient, and this opinion becomes general, almost the only method of averting or closing the calamities of war is lost.

Together with those maxims of universal equity which are common to states and individuals, there exists also amongst sovereigns a system of artificial jurisprudence, under the name of the *law of nations*.

Its rules derive their moral force simply from the general duty of conforming to the established regulations, but have all the virtue and obligation of a precept of natural justice.

War may be considered with a view to its *causes* and to its *conduct*.

The justifiable causes of it are deliberate invasion of right, and the necessity of maintaining the balance of power.

Whatever war has not for its motive, precaution, defence, or reparation, is unjustifiable.

There are two lessons of rational and sober policy, which would exclude many of the motives of war.

1. That princes should " place their glory, not in ex-
" tent of territory, but in raising the greatest portion of
" happiness out of a given territory."

Enlargement of territory is not only not a just object, but most frequently is not desireable from sound policy.

In two cases it may be of advantage both to the conquerors and to the conquered.

1st. Where an empire thereby reaches its natural boundaries.

2d. Where neighbouring states being severally too weak to defend themselves, can only be safe by a junction of their strength, which conquest effects.

3. That " national honour should never be pursued
" but on national interest."

The first case in which the honour of a nation is concerned, is that of interest.

But points of honour must be estimated with a reference to utility.

www.ingramcontent.com/pod-product-compliance
Lightning Source LLC
Chambersburg PA
CBHW081518040426

42447CB00013B/3261